THE ULTIMATE GUIDE TO ISO 27001
MASTERING INFORMATION SECURITY
MANAGEMENT
A Practical and Beginner-Friendly Approach to
the Latest ISO 27001 Standard
BY DANIEL SMITH

The Ultimate Guide to ISO 27001: Mastering Information Security Management

A Practical and Beginner-Friendly Approach to the Latest ISO 27001 Standard

By Daniel Smith

Copyright Page

Dedication Page

To all the businesses and professionals working to strengthen information security, protect data, and build trust. Your dedication to confidentiality, integrity, and availability doesn't just meet ISO 27001 — it raises the standard for everyone.

Introduction

In a world where cyberattacks, data leaks, and privacy failures can destroy a business overnight, protecting information is no longer optional — it's survival. ISO 27001 is the globally recognized standard that shows your organization takes information security seriously, not just in IT, but across people, processes, and technology.

The Ultimate Guide to ISO 27001: Mastering Information Security Management is written for beginners, managers, startup founders, and compliance teams who want clear direction without the usual dense, technical language. This book explains what ISO 27001 really is, why it matters, and how to implement it in a practical, step-by-step way.

You'll learn:

- How to build and manage an Information Security Management System (ISMS).
- How to identify and control security risks in your organization.
- What auditors actually look for during certification.
- How to turn security into trust, customer confidence, and competitive advantage.

This is not theory. It's a hands-on roadmap to the latest ISO 27001 standard — simplified. Whether you're trying to get certified or just want stronger security in your business, this book is designed to help you start, move forward, and lead.

About the Author

Daniel Smith is a recognized authority on international standards and management systems. With more than two decades of experience, he has supported organizations of all sizes in successfully achieving and maintaining certification.

Broad Expertise

His work spans a wide range of ISO standards, including quality management, information security, occupational health and safety, environmental management, and many others. This broad expertise allows him to offer guidance that is relevant across industries and business functions.

Practical and Clear Guidance

Through his books, toolkits, and resources, Daniel simplifies complex requirements into clear, step-by-step methods. His practical approach helps professionals move from theory to real-world application, ensuring compliance and measurable improvement.

Trusted Worldwide

Daniel's resources are trusted by managers, consultants, and business leaders around the world. His mission is to provide practical knowledge and tools that empower organizations to reduce risks, strengthen systems, and achieve sustainable success through certification.

Offer Information

Want to get the full document?

We are offering the Word document version of this book at **$20** for those who want to take the content with them wherever they go. For more information and to receive your copy, please contact us at:

Email: standardbookshub@gmail.com

Table of Contents

CHAPTER 1:

Introduction to ISO 27001

What is ISO 27001?

ISO 27001 is an international standard that defines the framework for establishing, implementing, maintaining, and continually improving an Information Security Management System (ISMS). It was developed by the International Organization for Standardization (ISO) in collaboration with the International Electrotechnical Commission (IEC) to help organizations manage the security of assets such as financial information, intellectual property, employee data, and information entrusted by third parties.

At its core, ISO 27001 provides a systematic approach to identifying potential security risks and applying appropriate controls to mitigate them. It helps organizations ensure the confidentiality, integrity, and availability of information—three principles that form the foundation of modern information security. By following this standard, an organization demonstrates its commitment to protecting data against unauthorized access, misuse, or loss.

The standard also emphasizes continuous improvement through regular audits, risk assessments, and reviews. This means that an organization certified under ISO 27001 is not only compliant at a single point in time but also committed to maintaining and enhancing its security posture over the long term. In a world where digital threats evolve rapidly, ISO 27001 serves as a trusted and globally recognized benchmark for building resilience and trust.

The Importance of Information Security

In today's interconnected world, information is one of the most valuable assets an organization possesses. Whether it involves customer details, trade secrets, or operational data, protecting information is essential to maintaining trust and ensuring smooth business operations. A single security breach can lead to significant financial losses, reputational damage, legal complications, and loss of customer confidence.

Information security is not just about technology; it is about people, processes, and awareness. Every organization relies on a combination of systems, employees, and policies to handle data responsibly. If even one element fails, sensitive information can be exposed. Therefore, building a strong culture of security is just as important as implementing technical defenses.

Furthermore, compliance with data protection laws and regulations—such as the General Data Protection Regulation (GDPR) or national cybersecurity acts—requires organizations to adopt structured approaches like ISO 27001. Beyond compliance, effective information security helps businesses operate confidently in digital environments, form partnerships, and expand globally.

In essence, protecting data is not merely a defensive act; it is a strategic necessity. It allows organizations to safeguard their reputation, maintain continuity, and create a foundation of trust with customers and stakeholders.

Impact of Data Breaches on Businesses

A data breach can be one of the most damaging events an organization faces. It occurs when unauthorized individuals gain access to confidential information, often exposing sensitive customer records, financial data, or proprietary business information. The impact of such incidents extends far beyond immediate financial loss; it can deeply affect an organization's reputation, operations, and long-term sustainability.

Financially, data breaches can lead to severe penalties, legal costs, and compensation claims from affected clients or partners. Companies may also incur expenses related to system recovery, cybersecurity improvements, and incident investigations. However, the financial aspect is often only the beginning of a much larger problem.

Reputation damage is perhaps the most enduring consequence. Once customers lose trust in an organization's ability to safeguard their information, rebuilding credibility can take years. Many businesses, especially small and medium enterprises, struggle to recover after a major breach due to the erosion of customer confidence and market value.

Operational disruption is another critical effect. In the aftermath of a breach, organizations often need to halt certain services, isolate compromised systems, and redirect resources toward damage control. This interruption can slow down business continuity, delay projects, and reduce productivity.

Moreover, data breaches can have long-term strategic implications. Competitors may exploit exposed data, trade secrets might lose their value, and regulators can impose stricter oversight. In sectors like finance, healthcare, and government, the implications of a breach can be especially grave, potentially putting national security or public safety at risk.

Ultimately, the impact of a data breach reminds organizations that information security is not optional. It is a fundamental business requirement and a key component of corporate resilience.

Key Concepts and Terminology

To understand ISO 27001 and the broader field of information security, it is essential to be familiar with certain key concepts and terms that form the foundation of the discipline.

Information Security Management System (ISMS):
The ISMS is a structured framework of policies, procedures, and controls designed to protect information assets. It enables organizations to identify risks, implement safeguards, and ensure continuous improvement.

Confidentiality, Integrity, and Availability (CIA):
These three principles are the cornerstones of information security. *Confidentiality* ensures that information is accessible only to authorized individuals. *Integrity* guarantees that data remains accurate and unaltered. *Availability* ensures that information and systems are accessible when needed.

Risk Assessment:

A systematic process used to identify potential threats, evaluate vulnerabilities, and determine the likelihood and impact of security incidents. It helps organizations prioritize resources and controls based on risk severity.

Control:

A control is any measure or safeguard—technical, administrative, or physical—implemented to reduce or eliminate security risks. Examples include firewalls, encryption, and access management policies.

Incident:

An event that compromises, or has the potential to compromise, information security. Incidents can range from phishing attacks and malware infections to data leaks or physical theft of devices.

Compliance:

Adherence to laws, regulations, and standards related to data protection. ISO 27001 helps organizations demonstrate compliance with international best practices.

Understanding these concepts creates the foundation upon which the entire ISO 27001 framework operates. They not only define the language of information security but also provide clarity and consistency when designing, implementing, and auditing an ISMS.

ISMS: Risk Management, Controls, and Audits

An effective Information Security Management System (ISMS) is built upon three essential pillars: **risk management, controls, and audits**. Together, they create a structured and verifiable framework that transforms abstract security policies into measurable performance. Each element serves a distinct but interconnected purpose—identifying risks, mitigating them through appropriate measures, and verifying that those measures work as intended.

Risk Management

Risk management lies at the heart of ISO 27001. It is the process that identifies potential threats to an organization's information assets, evaluates their likelihood and potential impact, and establishes measures to reduce those risks to acceptable levels.

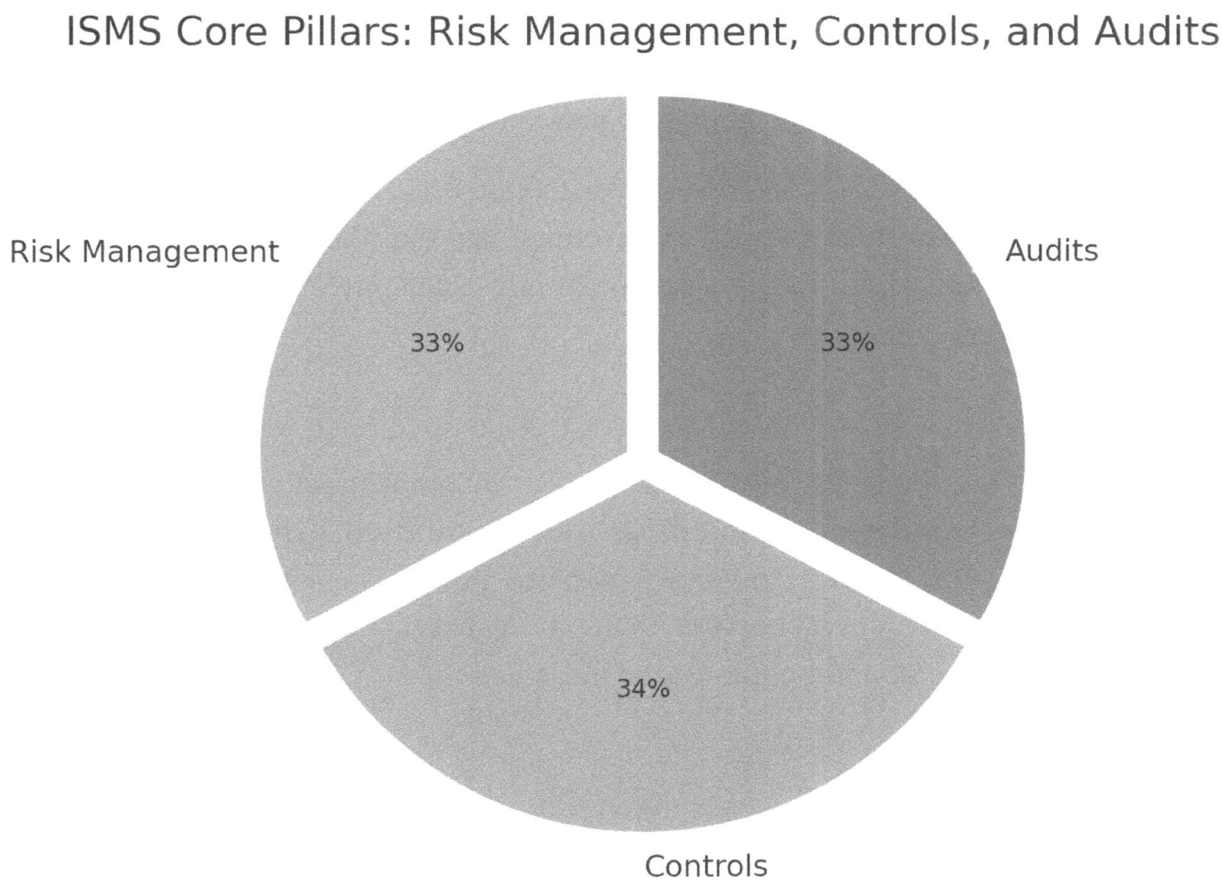

Rather than waiting for incidents to occur, ISO 27001 promotes a **proactive** approach—anticipating vulnerabilities before they cause damage.

The process begins by identifying the organization's **assets** (such as data, servers, laptops, applications, or personnel) and understanding how they could be compromised. Each asset is then analyzed for potential **threats** (like cyberattacks, hardware failure, or insider misuse) and **vulnerabilities** (weak passwords, outdated software, lack of encryption).

Next, the **likelihood** and **impact** of each risk are evaluated, usually on a numerical scale (for example, 1–5). The combination of these two factors determines the **risk level**, which helps prioritize mitigation efforts.

Mitigation may involve eliminating a risk (for example, by discontinuing an unsafe process), reducing it (by applying controls), transferring it (through insurance or outsourcing), or accepting it if it falls within acceptable limits. Importantly, risk management is a **continuous** activity—new risks emerge as the organization, technology, and environment evolve.

This process ensures that the ISMS focuses on the most significant threats, protecting resources where they matter most and maintaining business continuity even under adverse conditions.

Controls

Controls are the practical mechanisms used to implement risk management decisions. They represent the **defensive and preventive safeguards** that keep information secure. ISO 27001 outlines a detailed list of 93 controls (in its Annex A of the 2022 version), categorized across domains such as organizational, technological, physical, and people-based measures.

Controls can take several forms:

- **Technical controls**: firewalls, encryption, access control systems, multi-factor authentication.
- **Administrative controls**: policies, training programs, security procedures, and contractual clauses with vendors.
- **Physical controls**: locks, surveillance cameras, restricted areas, and visitor management.

Each control should be **chosen strategically**—not all controls apply to every organization. The choice depends on the specific risks identified during the assessment phase and on the organization's operational context, resources, and objectives.

Controls must also be **assigned to responsible personnel** with clear timelines for implementation. Regular reviews verify their effectiveness, and necessary adjustments are made to align with changing threats or business priorities.

In essence, controls translate the organization's commitment to information security into tangible, enforceable actions that safeguard confidentiality, integrity, and availability.

Audits

Audits ensure that the ISMS does not merely exist on paper but functions effectively in practice. ISO 27001 requires organizations to conduct **internal audits** at planned intervals to verify compliance, detect weaknesses, and identify opportunities for improvement.

An audit is not an inspection meant to assign blame—it is a **systematic evaluation** designed to strengthen the ISMS. Internal audits are typically carried out by trained employees who are independent of the areas being audited. External audits, conducted by certification bodies, validate compliance with the ISO 27001 standard and grant certification.

Auditors review documentation, interview staff, observe processes, and examine records to confirm that the ISMS meets both ISO requirements and the organization's own policies. If **non-conformities** are identified, they are documented and addressed through **corrective actions**, ensuring continual improvement.

An effective audit program increases transparency, accountability, and confidence. It reassures management, clients, and regulators that information security is not only designed but actively maintained and continually refined.

Professional Fillable Section for Practical Use

Concept	Explanation	Professional Fillable Section (for Practical Use)

Risk Management	Identifies potential threats to information assets, evaluates their likelihood and impact, and applies measures to reduce risks to acceptable levels. Risk management is proactive—it anticipates vulnerabilities before they cause harm and ensures continuous monitoring.	**Risk Assessment Table**• Asset Name: _________• Threat: _________• Vulnerability: _________• Likelihood (1–5): __ Impact (1–5): __• Control Applied: _________• Residual Risk: _________
Controls	Refers to technical, administrative, and physical safeguards that protect information from unauthorized access or misuse. Controls are selected based on the organization's specific risks and business needs, as outlined in Annex A of ISO 27001.	**Control Plan Table**• Control ID: _________• Description: _________• Responsible Person: _________• Implementation Date: _________• Status: _________
Audits	Involves systematic reviews to ensure the ISMS functions as intended. Internal and external audits verify compliance, identify weaknesses, and promote continuous improvement rather than punishment.	**Audit Record Table**• Audit Date: _________• Auditor Name: _________• Department Audited: _________• Findings: _________• Corrective Action: _________

Conclusion

Risk management identifies the battlefield, controls build the defenses, and audits ensure the defenses are holding strong. Together, these three components form the

operational core of ISO 27001—a dynamic cycle of identifying risks, applying controls, verifying results, and improving continuously.

Organizations that master this triad not only achieve certification but also gain lasting resilience, customer confidence, and a measurable competitive advantage in the digital landscape.

Benefits of ISO 27001

Enhancing Security and Compliance

Implementing ISO 27001 strengthens an organization's ability to protect sensitive information through a structured and proactive approach. It transforms information security from an IT-centric task into a company-wide responsibility. The standard helps identify vulnerabilities, assess risks, and apply targeted controls that reduce the likelihood of breaches or data loss.

In addition, ISO 27001 supports compliance with national and international regulations such as GDPR, HIPAA, or local data-protection laws. Organizations that align their practices with ISO 27001 demonstrate that they take legal obligations seriously and maintain transparent governance. This alignment not only minimizes regulatory risk but also avoids potential fines and operational disruption.

Building Trust with Customers and Stakeholders

Trust is the true currency of the digital age, and ISO 27001 certification serves as concrete evidence that an organization values and protects it. In a world where data breaches can destroy reputations within hours, certification reassures clients, partners, and regulators that information security is governed by internationally recognized standards rather than improvised practices. For customers, it offers the confidence that their personal and financial data is handled with care, transparency, and accountability—factors that directly influence loyalty and long-term engagement. For business partners and investors, ISO 27001 becomes proof of operational reliability and integrity, simplifying collaboration by reducing the need for repeated due-diligence reviews. In highly regulated fields such as finance, healthcare, and government, where confidentiality and trust are non-negotiable, this certification distinguishes an organization as a responsible and credible entity. It also strengthens relationships with regulators and investors by demonstrating structured governance, ongoing risk management, and adherence to legal obligations. Over time, the consistency and discipline required to maintain certification build a reputation of dependability that outlasts competitors. Thus, ISO 27001 is not merely a compliance badge—it is a strategic investment in credibility, transparency, and sustained trust in an interconnected digital economy.

Latest Updates in ISO 27001 (2022 Version)

The 2022 revision of ISO 27001 represents an important evolution in how organizations approach information security in a rapidly changing digital world. While the overall structure and intent of the standard remain consistent with the earlier version, the update refines the framework to better address the complexities of modern technologies, hybrid workplaces, and sophisticated cyber threats. One of the most significant changes lies in the restructuring of Annex A, where the previous 114 controls were streamlined into 93, now organized under four broad categories—organizational, people, physical, and technological controls. This thematic alignment reflects the reality that information security today is not confined to IT departments alone but involves people, culture, infrastructure, and governance. The reorganization improves clarity, removes overlap, and allows organizations to design more coherent and integrated control environments. The 2022 version also introduces 11 new controls to address previously underrepresented areas such as threat intelligence, data leakage prevention, web filtering, information deletion, monitoring of physical security, and secure configuration. These inclusions reflect the growing importance of proactive threat management, cloud-based data handling, and lifecycle security of digital assets. The update goes beyond technical adjustments—it reshapes the philosophy of ISO 27001 by encouraging organizations to adopt a risk-based and evidence-driven mindset. Greater emphasis is placed on continuous monitoring, performance evaluation, and integration with other management systems such as ISO 9001 (quality management) and ISO 22301 (business continuity management). This interconnected approach allows companies to align their security initiatives with broader operational and strategic goals, creating efficiency and consistency across compliance frameworks. Furthermore, the 2022 revision strengthens the link between technology and governance by recognizing that effective information security requires both robust systems and strong leadership. By blending adaptability with structure, the updated ISO 27001 standard provides organizations with a modern, flexible, and scalable framework—one capable of evolving alongside emerging technologies, shifting regulatory expectations, and increasingly complex cyber risks. In essence, this revision transforms ISO 27001 from a static compliance model into a dynamic management system that helps organizations remain secure, resilient, and competitive in a constantly changing digital landscape.

Topic	Explanation	Fillable Section (for Practical Use)
Enhancing Security and Compliance	Establishes structured defenses against information threats and ensures compliance with global data-protection laws. Demonstrates proactive risk management and legal accountability.	• Primary Risk Identified: __________• Control Implemented: __________• Compliance Standard: __________
Building Trust with Customers and Stakeholders	Strengthens reputation and credibility. Certification provides visible assurance of integrity, reliability, and confidentiality to all external parties.	• Client Group: __________• Trust Measure Used: __________• Expected Outcome: __________
ISO 27001 (2022 Version) Updates	Consolidated controls from 114 to 93 across 4 domains; introduced 11 new controls for cloud security and modern cyber threats; supports integration and continuous improvement.	• Updated Control Area: __________• Action Required: __________• Responsible Person: __________

Key Changes and Additions

The 2022 update of ISO 27001 was designed to bring the standard in line with the rapidly changing landscape of information security. While the foundation of risk-based management and continual improvement remains the same, the structure and scope of the controls were significantly modernized.

The most visible change is the reduction and reorganization of the controls listed in Annex A. The previous version, ISO 27001:2013, included 114 controls grouped under 14 domains. The 2022 revision consolidates them into 93 controls organized into four categories—Organizational, People, Physical, and Technological. This restructuring makes the standard easier to navigate and more adaptable to the needs of modern organizations.

Among the most notable additions are new controls that address today's evolving digital threats. These include controls for **threat intelligence, data leakage prevention, cloud services configuration, monitoring activities, web filtering, and secure deletion of information**. Each addition reflects the growing importance of data privacy, remote work, and cloud-based operations in business environments.

Another important enhancement is the alignment of ISO 27001 with the ISO Harmonized Structure (HLS), which allows it to integrate more smoothly with other management systems such as ISO 9001 (Quality Management) and ISO 22301 (Business Continuity). This integration simplifies the process for organizations that maintain multiple certifications by providing a unified structure for documentation, objectives, and audits.

How These Changes Impact Implementation

The 2022 revision has practical implications for how organizations design and maintain their Information Security Management Systems. The new structure encourages a more flexible, risk-driven approach rather than a checklist mentality. This means that organizations can tailor their security measures based on the relevance and severity of identified risks instead of following rigid procedural requirements.

By emphasizing the role of modern technologies and digital threats, the update ensures that organizations strengthen their defenses against cloud vulnerabilities, supply chain risks, and data leakage incidents. Implementation now requires closer collaboration between IT, compliance, and business leadership teams, fostering a culture of shared responsibility.

The consolidation of controls also streamlines audits and documentation. With fewer, better-organized controls, organizations can manage evidence more efficiently and reduce redundancy. Furthermore, the inclusion of new controls demands periodic reassessment of existing policies and training programs, ensuring that employees understand emerging risks and updated security expectations.

Overall, these changes transform ISO 27001 from a primarily compliance-focused system into a living framework that actively supports resilience, adaptability, and continual improvement.

ISO 27001 vs Other Standards

When comparing ISO 27001 with other major frameworks like **GDPR** and **NIST**, it becomes clear that while they share the common goal of protecting information, their focus and scope differ.

ISO 27001 is a comprehensive management system standard. It provides a systematic framework for establishing and maintaining information security across the entire organization. Its goal is to integrate security into business processes through continuous risk assessment, control implementation, and performance evaluation. It focuses on both strategic management and operational execution.

The **General Data Protection Regulation (GDPR)**, on the other hand, is a legal regulation enforced by the European Union. It focuses specifically on personal data protection and privacy rights. GDPR sets mandatory legal requirements for how organizations collect, process, and store personal information. While ISO 27001 helps organizations achieve compliance with GDPR by providing structure and controls, it is not a substitute for legal compliance. Instead, it serves as an enabler for meeting GDPR obligations in a consistent and auditable manner.

The **National Institute of Standards and Technology (NIST)** Cybersecurity Framework, developed in the United States, offers a set of best practices and guidelines rather than a certifiable standard. NIST emphasizes technical and operational controls within the domains of Identify, Protect, Detect, Respond, and Recover. Many organizations use NIST as a reference for designing specific technical safeguards, while ISO 27001 provides the overarching governance framework to manage those safeguards within a business context.

In essence, ISO 27001 defines *how* to build and manage an information security system, NIST guides *what* technical controls to apply, and GDPR dictates *why* certain protections are legally necessary. Together, they complement each other, creating a robust and balanced approach to information security and privacy.

Conclusion

ISO 27001 stands as one of the most comprehensive and practical standards for building trust, resilience, and accountability in the digital era. Its strength lies not only in setting rules but in creating a culture of continuous improvement where information security becomes part of everyday operations rather than an isolated technical function.

The 2022 revision modernizes the standard to address the realities of today's connected world—cloud computing, remote work, and evolving cyber threats. By reorganizing controls, introducing new ones, and aligning with other management systems, it ensures that organizations remain adaptable and forward-looking.

When compared with frameworks such as GDPR and NIST, ISO 27001 offers a unifying structure that connects compliance obligations, operational safeguards, and strategic management into a single, coherent system. It transforms information security from a defensive necessity into a competitive advantage—one that strengthens stakeholder confidence, supports regulatory compliance, and ensures long-term sustainability.

In essence, adopting ISO 27001 is not just about meeting a standard; it is about demonstrating integrity, foresight, and commitment to protecting what matters most—information.

CHAPTER 2:

The ISO 27001 Framework and Structure

Understanding the ISO 27001 Structure

ISO 27001 is built on a systematic framework designed to help organizations establish and maintain a robust Information Security Management System (ISMS). The standard follows the **Annex SL High-Level Structure**, a universal model adopted across all modern ISO management system standards. This alignment makes it easier for organizations to integrate ISO 27001 with other systems such as ISO 9001 for quality management or ISO 22301 for business continuity.

At its core, ISO 27001 consists of **10 main clauses**, followed by **Annex A**, which details specific security controls. The first three clauses—Scope, Normative References, and Terms and Definitions—are introductory and define the context of the standard. The remaining seven clauses form the operational and managerial backbone of ISO 27001.

Clauses 4 to 10 focus on how an organization should **plan, implement, evaluate, and improve** its information security processes. Clause 4 defines the **context of the organization**, ensuring that internal and external factors influencing security are identified. Clause 5 emphasizes **leadership and commitment**, requiring top management to take responsibility for security outcomes. Clause 6 introduces **planning and risk management**, a crucial step in identifying threats and determining appropriate controls.

Clause 7 deals with **support**, including resource allocation, staff competence, communication, and documentation. Clause 8 focuses on **operation**, where plans are executed and controls are implemented. Clause 9 outlines **performance evaluation**, emphasizing audits, monitoring, and measurement, while Clause 10 promotes **continuous improvement**, ensuring that the ISMS evolves as threats and technologies change.

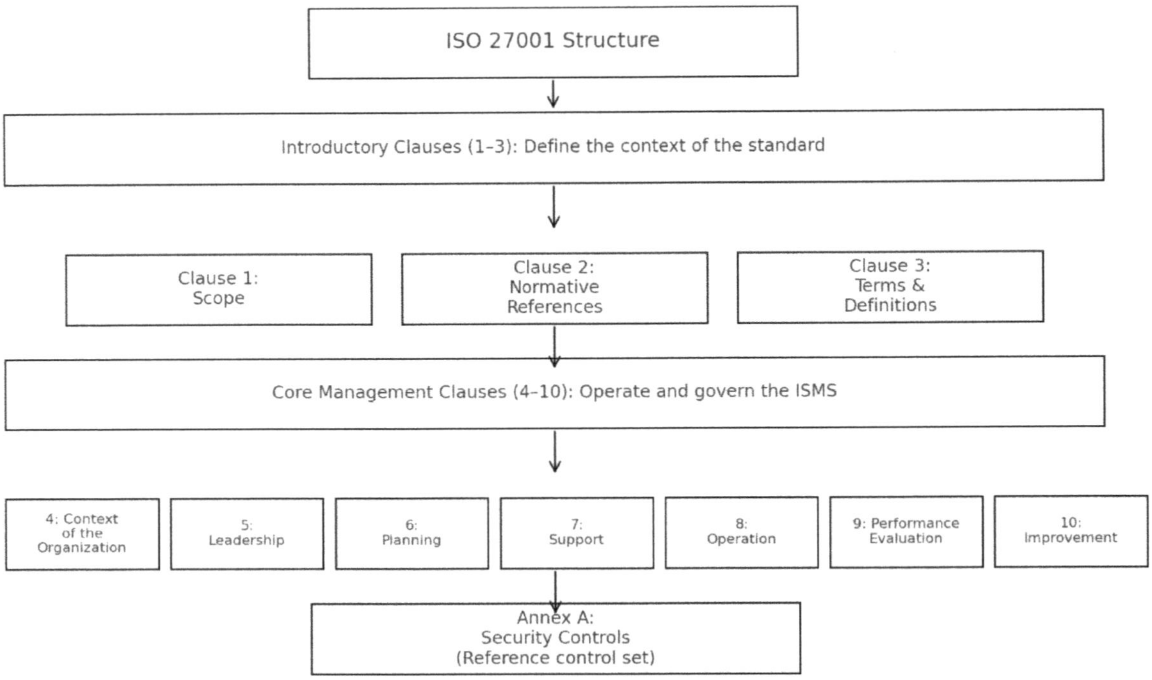

Explanation of Annex A (Controls)

Annex A is one of the most critical parts of ISO 27001. It contains a comprehensive list of **93 security controls**, organized into four main categories: **Organizational**, **People**, **Physical**, and **Technological controls**. These controls represent the practical measures organizations can adopt to reduce risks identified during their assessments.

The 2022 version of Annex A replaced the earlier 114 controls from the 2013 edition, streamlining and modernizing them to reflect current digital realities. For example, new controls have been added for **threat intelligence, cloud security, data masking, information deletion, and data leakage prevention**—areas that have become essential in the age of cloud computing and remote collaboration.

Each control in Annex A is not mandatory by default; instead, organizations must decide which controls are relevant to their risks and document their reasoning in a

Statement of Applicability (SoA). This flexibility ensures that the ISMS remains both efficient and tailored to the specific context of each organization.

Annex A, therefore, bridges the gap between theory and practice—it transforms high-level management objectives into concrete, actionable measures that strengthen data protection, operational stability, and regulatory compliance.

The Core Elements of an ISMS

The Information Security Management System (ISMS) represents the heart of ISO 27001. It is the structured combination of policies, processes, technologies, and people working together to protect information assets. An effective ISMS is built upon several core elements that ensure its sustainability and success.

The first element is **risk assessment and treatment**, where the organization identifies what information it needs to protect, evaluates potential threats, and decides how to mitigate them. This establishes a foundation for targeted, efficient security measures rather than broad, reactive ones.

The second element is **leadership and commitment**. ISO 27001 requires visible support from top management, as leadership sets the tone for organizational culture and accountability. Without management endorsement, even the most advanced security measures often fail due to lack of enforcement or awareness.

A third core element is **documented information**—the formal records that demonstrate compliance, define policies, and provide evidence of implementation. Proper documentation ensures consistency and transparency during audits and internal reviews.

Competence and awareness form another essential pillar. Employees at all levels must understand their security responsibilities, from handling sensitive data to recognizing phishing attempts. Ongoing training and awareness campaigns embed security into daily operations.

Lastly, the ISMS thrives on **continuous improvement**. Cyber threats evolve constantly, and so must the organization's defenses. Regular audits, monitoring, and corrective actions keep the ISMS dynamic and aligned with both internal growth and external challenges.

Together, these elements transform information security from a technical function into a management discipline that protects the organization's reputation, resources, and trust. The ISMS is not just a set of documents or tools—it is a living system that reflects the organization's values, resilience, and commitment to safeguarding information in an ever-changing world.

Understanding the Context of the Organization

Understanding the context of the organization is one of the most fundamental steps in establishing an effective Information Security Management System (ISMS). ISO 27001 begins with this requirement because it ensures that information security is not treated as a generic set of controls but as a tailored system shaped by the organization's unique environment, challenges, and objectives.

Context analysis provides the foundation on which every subsequent component of the ISMS is built—its scope, risk assessment, control selection, and continual improvement processes all depend on an accurate understanding of where the organization stands. Without it, even well-designed policies can miss their target, leading to inefficiency or wasted effort.

The standard divides this understanding into two primary dimensions: **internal** and **external** context.

Internal Context

The internal context defines the factors within the organization that influence how information security is managed and perceived. This includes the organization's structure, culture, existing policies, technological infrastructure, and overall capabilities.

The structure determines how decisions are made and who holds responsibility for security. A centralized organization may handle information security differently from a decentralized one with independent departments or branches. Understanding these dynamics helps assign roles and responsibilities clearly and ensures that controls fit within operational realities.

Culture plays an equally significant role. In organizations where security is seen as everyone's responsibility, compliance and awareness are naturally stronger. However, in environments where employees view security as an obstacle to productivity, controls may be bypassed or neglected. Assessing the prevailing culture allows leadership to design awareness programs and communication strategies that resonate with staff attitudes and behaviors.

Existing technology and resources must also be evaluated. The ISMS should be compatible with the current systems, tools, and processes in use. Knowing what technology supports business operations—whether it's legacy infrastructure, cloud systems, or third-party integrations—helps identify where risks may exist and what level of protection is feasible.

Internal context analysis, therefore, helps the organization understand its own capabilities and limitations. It enables the ISMS to be realistic and effective rather than idealistic or overly complex.

External Context

The external context involves the environmental, legal, regulatory, and social factors that affect the organization's approach to information security. These include compliance obligations, market conditions, customer expectations, competitive pressures, and the broader threat landscape.

Legal and regulatory requirements form a major part of the external context. Every organization operates under certain laws governing data protection, privacy, and industry-specific security obligations. For example, a healthcare institution may need to comply with patient confidentiality laws, while a financial institution must adhere to anti-fraud and data integrity regulations. Understanding these obligations ensures that the ISMS aligns with mandatory requirements and avoids legal exposure.

Stakeholder expectations are another critical consideration. Stakeholders include customers, employees, suppliers, regulators, investors, and even the general public. Each group has its own concerns—customers expect confidentiality, regulators demand compliance, and partners seek assurance of reliability. When these expectations are understood and incorporated into ISMS objectives, the organization builds trust and demonstrates accountability.

Market conditions and technological trends also influence the external context. As digital transformation accelerates, organizations face new forms of risk—cyberattacks, data breaches, and supply chain vulnerabilities. External context analysis allows the organization to stay aware of such emerging threats and to adapt its security strategy accordingly.

By mapping both the risks and opportunities in the external environment, the organization ensures that its ISMS remains forward-looking and responsive rather than static.

Aligning Context with ISMS Objectives

Defining the context of the organization is not a one-time or isolated step—it is the strategic cornerstone that determines how effectively information security aligns with business goals. ISO 27001 emphasizes this concept because an Information Security Management System (ISMS) cannot operate successfully in a vacuum. It must be built around the organization's real-world environment, challenges, and ambitions. When leaders clearly understand both internal and external factors, they can create security objectives that are not only realistic but also purposeful, measurable, and directly tied to business priorities. In essence, context transforms the ISMS from a compliance-driven framework into a strategic management tool that actively supports growth, innovation, and resilience.

For many organizations, defining context begins with a deep reflection on **why** they exist and **what** they seek to protect. Information security should serve as a foundation that enables business performance rather than as a constraint that slows progress. When context is well-understood, security initiatives complement the organization's direction instead of competing with it. For example, a technology company expanding into digital services must recognize that its external context now involves greater exposure to cyberattacks, data privacy regulations, and global supply chain dependencies. Understanding this expanded risk environment naturally leads to meaningful ISMS objectives such as strengthening network security controls, conducting regular vulnerability assessments, training employees in cybersecurity awareness, and establishing stronger incident response procedures. Each of these actions directly supports the business's ability to scale safely and maintain customer trust.

On the other hand, internal context focuses on what the organization can realistically achieve with its current structure, resources, and capabilities. A small or medium-sized enterprise, for instance, may identify constraints such as limited IT staff, budgetary restrictions, or reliance on outdated systems. Recognizing these internal limitations is not a weakness—it is an opportunity for intelligent planning. Instead of pursuing costly or overly complex security measures, leadership can prioritize gradual improvements, such as automating basic controls, outsourcing specialized security functions, or adopting cost-effective cloud-based solutions. By aligning security objectives with available capacity, the ISMS remains sustainable, achievable, and continuously improving rather than becoming an unrealistic administrative burden.

A clearly defined context also ensures that risk management efforts focus on what truly matters. Organizations often face hundreds of potential risks, but not all of them require equal attention. By understanding the business landscape and identifying critical assets—such as customer data, intellectual property, or operational systems—leaders can allocate resources efficiently and concentrate on the most significant threats. This clarity allows the ISMS to act as a precision instrument rather than a broad checklist, delivering measurable value and supporting informed decision-making.

Beyond immediate benefits, context-setting builds **organizational resilience**. Businesses today operate in environments characterized by constant technological evolution, shifting regulatory requirements, and unpredictable global events. A well-defined context prepares the ISMS to adapt to these changes by regularly revisiting assumptions, reviewing external trends, and updating internal priorities. For instance, the sudden rise of remote work or new data protection laws can dramatically alter an organization's risk profile. When context is treated as an ongoing process rather than a one-time task, the ISMS evolves alongside the business instead of lagging behind it.

Moreover, defining context promotes **a culture of security awareness** throughout the organization. When employees at all levels understand the broader business and risk environment, they can make decisions that align with both operational goals and security objectives. Security then becomes part of daily work habits rather than a separate compliance requirement. This integration of culture, process, and strategy strengthens trust internally and externally, positioning the organization as both secure and forward-looking.

Ultimately, the value of defining context lies in its ability to connect every element of ISO 27001—from leadership commitment and risk assessment to control implementation and continual improvement—under a unified vision. It ensures that the ISMS is strategically aligned, practically grounded, and resilient to disruption. When context is clearly understood and regularly reviewed, information security becomes not just a protective mechanism but a **strategic enabler**—allowing the organization to innovate confidently, build stakeholder trust, and sustain long-term success in an increasingly complex digital world.

Conclusion

In summary, understanding the context of the organization transforms ISO 27001 from a set of rules into a customized framework for long-term success. It ensures that every control, process, and policy reflects real-world conditions—how the organization operates, what it values, and what it must protect.

When internal and external factors are properly analyzed, the ISMS becomes not just a compliance tool but a strategic asset—one that safeguards information, strengthens reputation, and supports sustainable growth in a world of constant change.

Leadership and Planning Requirements

Strong leadership forms the cornerstone of every effective Information Security Management System (ISMS). ISO 27001 places explicit accountability on top management to set the tone, direction, and culture of security within the organization. The standard makes it clear that leadership is not a symbolic role—it is an operational responsibility. Executives must establish the organization's security policy, define objectives, and ensure that adequate resources, competencies, and communication channels are in place to implement them.

True leadership in information security goes beyond approving documents. It requires visible engagement. When top management actively participates in reviews, training sessions, and incident evaluations, it sends a clear message throughout the organization that security is a shared priority, not an isolated technical concern. This visible commitment influences employee behavior more effectively than any written policy could. When staff see leadership following procedures, attending awareness meetings, or asking informed questions about risk, they are far more likely to take their own responsibilities seriously.

Accountability is equally important. Leaders must assign clear roles and responsibilities to ensure that every control within the ISMS has an owner. Accountability does not mean blame—it means ownership and empowerment. When responsibilities are well-defined, decision-making becomes faster, coordination improves, and controls are implemented with precision.

Leadership also extends to ensuring that information security aligns with broader organizational objectives. Security cannot exist in a vacuum; it must support business strategy, protect assets that matter most, and enable growth. A well-integrated ISMS allows innovation and efficiency to flourish without compromising protection. This balance—between enabling business and managing risk—is one of the most valuable contributions leadership can make.

Support and Operational Needs

Support and operations represent the practical backbone of an Information Security Management System (ISMS). Leadership and planning define direction, but it is support and operations that make those directions sustainable and functional in daily life. ISO 27001 dedicates considerable attention to these two areas because they determine whether the system truly works or remains only theoretical.

Support: The Foundation of an Effective ISMS

Support encompasses the resources, infrastructure, and culture that sustain information security. Without proper support, even the most carefully designed

ISMS cannot operate effectively. ISO 27001 requires organizations to ensure that people are competent, that communication is reliable, and that documentation is controlled and accessible.

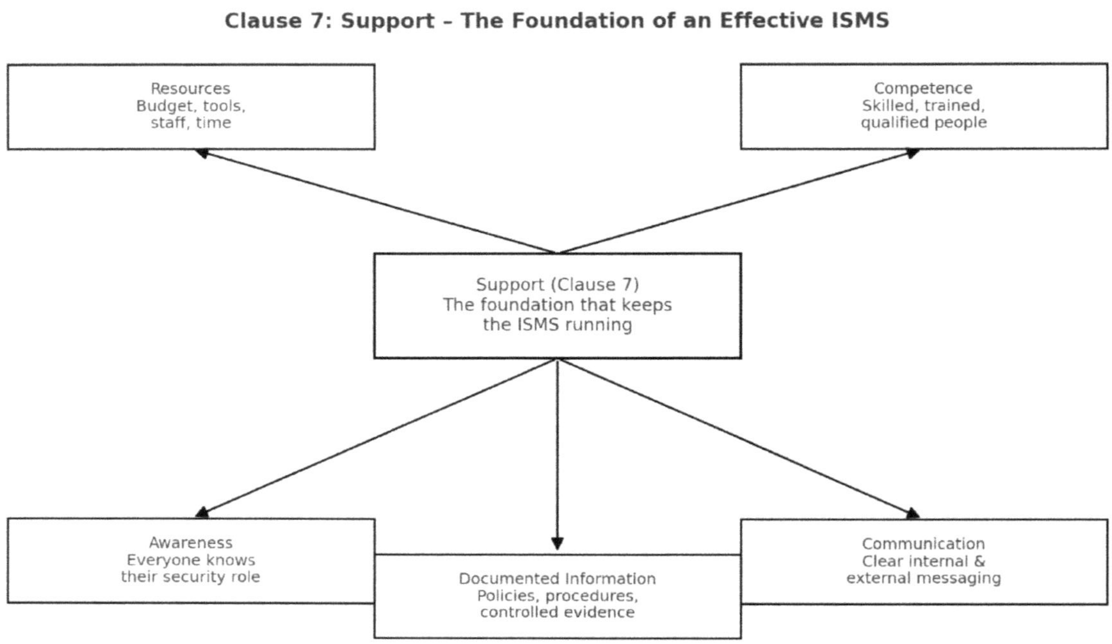

People form the core of support. The standard emphasizes that every individual involved in information processing must have the necessary knowledge, skills, and awareness to perform their role securely. Competence is not limited to technical expertise—it includes understanding policies, recognizing threats, and responding appropriately to incidents. Regular training, workshops, and awareness programs are essential to maintain this competence. When employees understand why controls exist, compliance becomes a shared responsibility rather than a forced obligation.

Technology is another critical element of support. The organization must maintain secure, reliable systems that protect data integrity, availability, and confidentiality. This includes not only hardware and software but also secure network infrastructure, backup systems, and access control mechanisms. The technology should be appropriate for the organization's scale and complexity, with regular maintenance and updates to prevent vulnerabilities.

Communication ties these components together. ISO 27001 stresses the importance of both internal and external communication channels. Internally, employees must know whom to contact in case of security incidents, how to report risks, and where to find relevant policies. Externally, communication ensures that clients, partners, and regulators receive accurate information about the organization's security commitments when necessary. A failure in communication can lead to misunderstandings, delayed responses, and reputational damage.

Documentation completes the support framework. Every process, control, and policy must be properly documented, reviewed, and version-controlled. Documentation ensures continuity—especially when staff change roles or systems evolve. It also serves as verifiable evidence during audits, demonstrating that controls are implemented as intended. The key to effective documentation is balance: it should be detailed enough to ensure clarity but concise enough to remain practical and usable.

Operations: Turning Plans into Practice

If support provides the foundation, operations bring the ISMS to life. This is the stage where plans, policies, and risk treatments are implemented in real terms. ISO 27001 expects organizations to establish structured processes for executing and managing security activities in a consistent, measurable way.

Operations begin with the implementation of controls identified in the risk treatment plan. These controls may include access restrictions, encryption, supplier assessments, or incident response mechanisms. Each control must be documented, assigned to responsible personnel, and regularly reviewed to confirm effectiveness. Controls should never exist in isolation—they must work together to mitigate identified risks.

Monitoring is an integral part of operations. The organization must continuously observe performance indicators, system logs, and incident data to verify that controls are working as expected. Regular monitoring helps detect anomalies early and provides valuable data for improvement. This is where the ISMS moves from being reactive to being preventive—problems are anticipated and addressed before they cause damage.

Incident management is another key operational responsibility. Despite all preventive measures, security incidents can still occur. The organization must have clear, rehearsed procedures for identifying, reporting, and responding to these events. Every incident should be logged, analyzed, and resolved with corrective action. Lessons learned from incidents feed back into risk assessments and help strengthen the overall ISMS.

Operations also involve ensuring business continuity. ISO 27001 connects information security with operational resilience. Plans for data recovery, alternate communication, and emergency response must be in place so that critical services can continue even under disruption. Consistent testing of these plans ensures they remain effective when needed most.

Documentation within operations must remain current. Records of access logs, patch management, vulnerability scans, and audit trails form the evidence that controls are not only designed but actively working. This documentation supports accountability and enables traceability during audits.

In essence, operations transform security strategy into daily discipline. They ensure that what leadership envisions and what planning outlines actually happen on the ground.

The Connection Between Support and Operations

Support and operations are two pillars that sustain the effectiveness of an Information Security Management System (ISMS). They are not independent components but interconnected forces that depend on each other to function properly. Support provides the essential foundation—the people, resources, tools, infrastructure, and communication systems that make implementation possible—while operations bring those resources to life by turning plans into consistent, measurable actions. One without the other cannot deliver a mature or reliable ISMS.

When support is weak, even the best-designed operations begin to falter. Without competent staff, adequate tools, or clear documentation, security processes become inconsistent and error-prone. Employees may not fully understand their roles, systems may be misconfigured, and policies may be applied unevenly across departments. On the other hand, when operations lack structure or discipline, even strong support cannot achieve long-term success. Investments in training, technology, and awareness lose their impact if they are not channeled through well-defined operational procedures. The absence of coordination and follow-up creates gaps that weaken the entire security posture.

True effectiveness arises when support and operations function harmoniously. In such organizations, leadership ensures that employees have both the competence and motivation to carry out their security responsibilities. The tools provided are not just technically advanced but also suited to the organization's needs and workflows. Communication flows openly across teams—technical staff, management, and external stakeholders all understand how their roles interconnect within the ISMS. This open communication minimizes confusion and ensures quick, coordinated responses during security incidents.

When the two elements align, the ISMS transforms from a static set of rules into a **living system**. It adapts dynamically to new technologies, evolving threats, and organizational changes. For instance, when a new business application is introduced or a remote work policy is implemented, the ISMS automatically adjusts—through updated risk assessments, revised access controls, and refresher training programs. This adaptability ensures that information security remains relevant and integrated into every level of organizational activity rather than isolated within the IT department.

Such harmony also promotes confidence. Employees understand not just what to do, but why it matters. They recognize that their actions contribute directly to protecting the organization's information assets and reputation. This sense of ownership strengthens compliance naturally, without the need for excessive enforcement. Managers, meanwhile, gain visibility into performance through regular monitoring, reporting, and internal audits, allowing them to make timely improvements.

Over time, the synergy between support and operations builds a cycle of continual improvement—the hallmark of ISO 27001. Each audit, incident report, or performance review feeds into enhanced processes, better training, and more refined controls. The organization becomes resilient, capable of withstanding disruptions and learning from them.

In essence, the interdependence of support and operations represents the operational heart of ISO 27001. Support empowers people and equips them to act; operations channel that energy into structured, consistent security practices. Together, they create an ecosystem where policies are practiced, technology is trusted, and incidents are managed with precision. This integration forms the true strength behind ISO 27001 compliance—a living, responsive, and continually improving system that upholds not just security, but the long-term stability and credibility of the entire organization.

Performance Evaluation and Improvement

No **management system** can remain truly effective without **ongoing evaluation**. In ISO 27001, continuous assessment is not optional—it is a core requirement that keeps the **Information Security Management System (ISMS)** relevant, efficient, and aligned with business objectives. Evaluation ensures that the organization does not fall into a pattern of static compliance but instead develops a culture of **accountability, learning, and improvement**.

ISO 27001 demands a structured process of **performance evaluation**, involving **audits, management reviews, and data-driven analysis**. Each of these elements serves a distinct yet complementary purpose. **Internal audits** act as a reality check; they confirm whether security controls are working as intended and whether employees are following established procedures. These audits help uncover inefficiencies, overlooked vulnerabilities, or deviations from policy before they escalate into serious risks. They are designed not to punish but to **verify, validate, and improve**.

Meanwhile, **management reviews** take a broader, strategic view. Senior leadership evaluates whether the ISMS continues to support the organization's mission and goals, and whether its performance indicators remain relevant in light of evolving business priorities. During these reviews, leaders examine audit results, incident reports, and key performance data to determine whether resources, staffing, or policies require adjustment. This top-level oversight ensures that **information**

security remains integrated with business direction rather than being treated as an isolated technical activity.

The process of **improvement** naturally follows evaluation. ISO 27001 treats improvement not as a corrective reaction but as a **continuous cycle** of learning and adaptation. Whenever weaknesses are identified—whether through an incident, an audit finding, or employee feedback—organizations are required to implement **corrective actions** promptly. These actions might include revising a control, retraining staff, upgrading technology, or updating a policy. The emphasis is on addressing the **root cause** rather than merely fixing the symptom.

Continuous improvement ensures that the ISMS does not stagnate. It evolves alongside **technological advancements**, **organizational restructuring**, and **regulatory updates**, maintaining its strength and relevance over time. This adaptability is especially critical in today's environment, where new threats and vulnerabilities emerge almost daily. A system that learns from experience and adjusts its controls accordingly is one that sustains **resilience and credibility**.

By embedding evaluation and improvement into daily operations, organizations cultivate a mindset of vigilance and progress. Employees come to view audits and reviews not as interruptions but as opportunities for refinement. Management, in turn, gains confidence that the ISMS remains aligned with both operational performance and strategic vision.

Risk-Based Approach to Information Security

At the **heart of ISO 27001** lies the **risk-based approach**, a principle that defines how modern information security should function. Unlike rigid compliance systems that prescribe identical controls for every organization, ISO 27001 emphasizes **flexibility and proportionality**. It requires each organization to **identify, assess, and treat risks** according to its own **unique context**, acknowledging that every business operates under different conditions, resources, and levels of exposure. This approach makes the standard both **universal and adaptable**, ensuring that information security remains practical and effective rather than bureaucratic.

The **risk-based approach** recognizes that **information security is not one-size-fits-all**. A multinational bank faces very different threats from a small design firm, yet both need to protect their information assets in a manner that reflects their **specific objectives and vulnerabilities**. The goal is not to implement every possible control, but to apply the **right controls** in the **right places** to achieve the desired level of protection.

The process begins with a structured **risk assessment**, the foundation of every ISMS. This involves **identifying critical assets** that require protection—such as customer databases, financial systems, proprietary research, or operational technology. Each of these assets carries a different level of sensitivity and value. Once identified, the organization evaluates **potential threats** (like cyberattacks, human error, data theft, or natural disasters) and **vulnerabilities** (such as weak passwords, outdated software, or poor access control). The next step is to determine the **likelihood** of each threat exploiting a vulnerability and the **impact** it would have if it occurred. These two dimensions—likelihood and impact—combine to define the **level of risk**, allowing organizations to prioritize which issues need immediate attention and which can be monitored over time.

After assessing the risks, the organization moves to **risk treatment**, selecting and implementing appropriate **controls** to mitigate or reduce risks to an **acceptable level**. ISO 27001 does not dictate which controls to use; instead, it provides a structured reference (Annex A) from which organizations can choose measures that align with their needs. This flexibility ensures that small companies are not overburdened with unnecessary requirements, while larger enterprises can deploy more complex and layered protections. The objective is to achieve **risk reduction**, not absolute elimination—because zero risk is impossible, but managed risk is achievable.

One of the great strengths of this approach is its focus on **efficiency and adaptability**. By aligning controls with the most significant risks, organizations allocate resources wisely, avoiding wasted effort on low-impact issues. Regular **risk reviews** ensure that the ISMS remains current as new technologies, threats, and business processes emerge. For example, when an organization adopts **cloud computing** or **remote work models**, its risk profile changes dramatically; the risk-based approach allows it to adjust quickly by reassessing vulnerabilities and updating controls.

Beyond operational benefits, the **risk-based approach** fosters a **strategic mindset**. It links **information security directly to business continuity, resilience, and performance**. Instead of viewing security as a defensive cost, organizations begin to see it as an **enabler of stability and trust**—a framework that protects what drives their success. This alignment between security and strategy is what distinguishes ISO 27001 from traditional compliance programs.

Ultimately, the **risk-based approach** transforms ISO 27001 from a checklist into a **living management system**. It encourages continual learning, regular reassessment, and proactive decision-making. By integrating risk thinking into everyday operations, organizations not only achieve compliance but also build **long-term agility, resilience, and competitive strength** in an environment where cyber threats evolve faster than ever before.

Area	**Purpose / Explanation**	**To Be Filled by Reader / Organization**
Context of Organization	Identify internal and external factors that influence information security.	• Internal Factors: __________ • External Factors: __________ • Interested Parties: __________
Leadership & Planning	Define objectives, assign roles, and set measurable security goals.	• ISMS Objective: __________ • Responsible Leader: __________ • Target Date: __________
Performance & Risk Review	Evaluate ISMS performance and document key risks with actions for improvement.	• Key Risk Identified: __________ • Control Applied: __________ • Improvement Action: __________

Identifying and Assessing Risks

An effective Information Security Management System begins with a thorough understanding of risk. In ISO 27001, risk is defined as the possibility that a threat will exploit a vulnerability, leading to the loss of confidentiality, integrity, or availability of information. Identifying and assessing these risks ensures that an organization can make informed decisions about where to allocate resources and which controls to prioritize.

The process starts with establishing a **risk assessment methodology**—a consistent approach to determine how risks are recognized, measured, and treated. This methodology defines key elements such as the organization's risk acceptance criteria, evaluation scale (for likelihood and impact), and review frequency.

During risk identification, all valuable information assets are documented along with their owners, locations, and dependencies. Threats may range from cyberattacks and insider misuse to power failures or natural disasters. Vulnerabilities, on the other hand, might include weak access controls, outdated software, or human error.

Once identified, each risk is evaluated for **likelihood** (how probable it is to occur) and **impact** (how severe the consequences would be if it occurred). These values are combined to determine a **risk score**, which helps prioritize action. The result is a clear, data-driven picture of the organization's security landscape.

Risk Treatment and Mitigation

Risk assessment alone is not enough; organizations must decide how to respond to each identified risk. ISO 27001 outlines four possible treatment strategies: **avoid**, **transfer**, **mitigate**, or **accept**.

- *Avoidance* involves discontinuing the activity that generates the risk.
- *Transfer* may include purchasing cyber-insurance or outsourcing specific processes.
- *Mitigation* focuses on applying controls—such as encryption, firewalls, or awareness training—to reduce the likelihood or impact.

- *Acceptance* is used when the cost or effort of further reduction outweighs the benefit.

For each risk, an organization documents its chosen strategy in a **Risk Treatment Plan**, detailing the actions required, responsible personnel, and implementation deadlines. These actions are then tracked to ensure they are completed and reviewed for effectiveness.

The purpose of risk treatment is not to eliminate all risks—an impossible goal—but to achieve a level of exposure that aligns with the organization's tolerance and strategic objectives. A well-managed risk process transforms uncertainty into structured decision-making, reinforcing both operational stability and stakeholder confidence.

The Role of Leadership in ISO 27001

Importance of Executive Buy-In

Leadership commitment is the cornerstone of ISO 27001 success. Without visible and active support from senior management, even the most well-designed policies struggle to gain traction. Executive buy-in ensures that information security is not treated as a technical concern limited to the IT department, but as a strategic business priority.

Leaders are responsible for setting the tone of accountability, allocating resources, and defining security objectives that align with the organization's broader goals. When executives actively participate in reviews, approve budgets, and communicate the importance of compliance, they establish a culture in which information security becomes everyone's responsibility.

Moreover, regulatory bodies and auditors look for evidence of leadership involvement—policies signed by executives, management review minutes, and documented objectives—to confirm genuine organizational commitment. A lack of leadership engagement is one of the most common reasons ISO 27001 implementations fail to deliver long-term value.

How Leadership Drives Success in ISO 27001 Implementation

Effective leadership does more than approve initiatives; it **drives continuous improvement**. Leaders define the vision for the ISMS, ensure its alignment with business objectives, and provide the authority necessary to enforce security measures. They also foster communication across departments, encouraging collaboration between IT, HR, legal, and operations.

Successful leaders establish measurable objectives—such as reducing incidents, increasing compliance scores, or improving audit performance—and monitor progress through regular reporting. They promote transparency by recognizing achievements and addressing weaknesses constructively.

Ultimately, leadership transforms ISO 27001 from a compliance exercise into a strategic advantage. When management integrates information security into business decisions, product design, and customer engagement, the ISMS becomes a living framework that supports trust, innovation, and growth.

Customizing ISO 27001 to Fit Your Organization

Adapting the Framework to Your Business Needs

While **ISO 27001 provides a universal structure**, it is intentionally designed to be **flexible and adaptable**. The standard establishes *what* must be achieved but leaves the *how* to the discretion of each organization. This flexibility is crucial because no two organizations share identical environments, risk exposures, or operational capacities. A government agency, a small consultancy, and a multinational corporation can all implement ISO 27001, but the way they apply its principles will vary dramatically. The **framework must be tailored** to reflect each entity's **size, complexity, risk appetite, and industry-specific requirements**.

Customization begins with a deep understanding of the **organizational context**—the foundation upon which the Information Security Management System (ISMS) rests. Organizations must determine **which assets hold the greatest value**, such as customer data, proprietary designs, or financial systems. They must also identify **which threats are most likely** to affect them, whether from cyberattacks, insider misuse, or environmental events. Once this context is defined, the organization can determine what level of **security control is both necessary and sustainable**. This ensures that the ISMS protects what truly matters without consuming resources unnecessarily.

For example, a **hospital** implementing ISO 27001 would naturally focus on protecting **patient data**, maintaining compliance with **healthcare regulations**, and ensuring the **availability of critical medical systems**. Confidentiality and regulatory alignment would be its highest priorities. In contrast, a **software company** may prioritize **intellectual property protection**, **secure code development**, and **cloud infrastructure security**, where uptime and integrity take precedence. Both organizations operate under the same ISO 27001 structure, yet their **risk treatment strategies, control selection, and documentation depth** differ because their environments and responsibilities are not the same.

The essence of customization lies in **relevance**. Every control within the ISMS should have a **clear and justifiable purpose**, directly supporting a defined **business objective** or mitigating a **specific risk**. Controls should never be implemented merely because they appear in the standard or seem technically sophisticated. Instead, they should form a cohesive and efficient system that aligns information security with organizational goals. This targeted approach reduces redundancy, simplifies management, and ensures that resources are spent where they create the greatest value.

Customization also extends beyond technical measures—it applies equally to **documentation, governance, and processes**. A **large enterprise** with complex hierarchies and multiple departments might require **formalized policies, detailed reporting mechanisms, and dedicated review committees** to maintain oversight. Conversely, a **small business** or startup might achieve the same objectives through **streamlined procedures, concise policies, and direct communication channels**. What matters is not the volume of documentation but its **clarity, accuracy, and applicability**. ISO 27001 explicitly discourages unnecessary bureaucracy, promoting a "**fit-for-purpose**" approach to compliance. The standard's goal is **effectiveness, not paperwork**—it values how well the system functions over how thick the manuals are.

Moreover, customization ensures that the ISMS remains **scalable**. As an organization grows, enters new markets, or adopts new technologies, the ISMS should evolve accordingly. Policies and controls must be flexible enough to expand without needing complete redesign. For instance, when a company transitions from on-premises servers to a cloud environment, the ISMS should easily integrate new cloud-specific controls, vendor management processes, and data protection measures without disrupting existing operations.

Another key advantage of tailoring ISO 27001 is **employee engagement**. When the framework reflects the organization's real processes, employees find it more practical and relatable. Overly rigid or generic systems often fail because they feel imposed rather than integrated. A customized ISMS, on the other hand, resonates with staff responsibilities and workflows, making compliance intuitive and sustainable.

Ultimately, **customization transforms ISO 27001 from a compliance checklist into a living management system**—one that adapts to the organization's realities and enhances rather than hinders business performance. The flexibility built into the standard allows it to serve organizations of every scale, from small startups to global enterprises, by ensuring that information security remains aligned with business purpose, operational efficiency, and long-term strategic growth.

Flexibility and Scalability of the Standard

One of **ISO 27001's greatest strengths** lies in its inherent **flexibility and scalability**. Unlike rigid compliance frameworks that impose the same structure on every organization, ISO 27001 was intentionally designed to accommodate businesses of all sizes, sectors, and levels of technological maturity. Whether applied to a **multinational corporation** managing complex digital infrastructures or a **small startup** just beginning its security journey, the core principles of ISO 27001 remain equally relevant and practical.

The **scalability** of ISO 27001 allows organizations to grow into compliance at a sustainable pace. Many businesses start small—identifying their **most critical information assets**, establishing foundational controls, and defining a limited scope for their ISMS. As their **resources, staff expertise, and technological maturity** increase, they can gradually expand the scope, strengthen risk management practices, and introduce more sophisticated controls. This incremental growth model prevents organizations from being overwhelmed and ensures that implementation remains both manageable and meaningful.

The **flexible structure** of ISO 27001 also ensures that compliance is achievable regardless of industry or budget. The standard's **risk-based approach** means that controls are selected based on actual business exposure rather than a checklist mentality. A financial institution, for example, might invest heavily in encryption and fraud detection systems, while a manufacturing company may prioritize physical security and supply chain controls. Both remain compliant because their ISMS reflects their **specific risk environments** and operational realities.

Another major advantage of ISO 27001's flexibility is its ability to **integrate with other management systems**, such as **ISO 9001 (Quality Management)**, **ISO 22301 (Business Continuity)**, or **ISO 20000 (IT Service Management)**. This integration allows organizations to build a **unified governance framework** that streamlines documentation, reduces duplication, and improves overall efficiency. For example, risk assessments conducted for ISO 27001 can inform business continuity strategies under ISO 22301, creating synergy between departments and aligning security with broader business objectives.

Furthermore, ISO 27001 demonstrates exceptional adaptability to **emerging technologies and evolving work models**. As businesses adopt **artificial intelligence**, **cloud computing**, **Internet of Things (IoT)**, or **remote collaboration tools**, the standard remains relevant because it focuses on principles rather than prescriptive methods. Its **risk-based thinking** ensures that as new technologies introduce novel threats, organizations can identify, evaluate, and control them without needing to reinvent their ISMS. This adaptability keeps ISO 27001 **modern, forward-looking, and resilient**, even in the face of rapid digital transformation.

Flexibility also extends to the **documentation and governance style** an organization chooses. Large enterprises may rely on extensive formal policies, detailed risk registers, and structured approval workflows. Smaller businesses, however, can maintain compliance using concise procedures, clear responsibilities, and direct communication lines. ISO 27001 does not measure success by the number of documents created but by the **effectiveness of the system in managing information security risks**. This approach ensures that the framework remains accessible and meaningful to organizations at every stage of their development.

When supported by **strong leadership commitment**, ISO 27001 becomes more than a security framework—it evolves into a **strategic enabler** of organizational excellence. It fosters a culture of accountability, drives process improvement, and reinforces stakeholder trust by proving that information is handled responsibly. Over time, this combination of structure and flexibility empowers organizations to respond swiftly to change while maintaining consistent control over their information assets.

Conclusion

In essence, **ISO 27001 is not a static rulebook but a dynamic framework**—one that matures alongside the organization it serves. Its scalability allows small businesses to start with essential protections and large enterprises to fine-tune global risk management systems, all under the same standard. Its flexibility makes it compatible with new technologies, diverse industries, and evolving regulatory landscapes. This balance between structure and adaptability ensures that ISO 27001 remains timeless: a living system capable of **defending against present threats while preparing for future ones**. When implemented thoughtfully, guided by clear leadership and a culture of continual improvement, ISO 27001 becomes both a **shield that safeguards organizational integrity** and a **catalyst that drives sustained performance, resilience, and trust**.

CHAPTER 3:

Implementing ISO 27001 in Your Organization

Laying the Foundation for ISO 27001

Implementing **ISO 27001** is not merely a technical undertaking; it represents a **strategic transformation** that reshapes how an organization thinks, operates, and manages risk. It goes beyond deploying firewalls, policies, or encryption—it is about embedding **security into the organizational DNA** so that every decision, process, and interaction reflects a commitment to protecting information. This transformation requires alignment between technology, people, and processes, ensuring that information security becomes not just an IT function but a **core business value** that supports trust, efficiency, and long-term sustainability.

The **foundation phase** of ISO 27001 implementation plays a decisive role in determining the success of the entire initiative. It sets the **vision, structure, and priorities** that guide every subsequent stage of development. At this stage, organizations must define the **scope of their ISMS**, identifying which assets, departments, or systems fall within its boundaries. They also establish **governance mechanisms**, such as assigning responsibilities to information security officers, defining escalation paths, and forming internal committees to oversee progress. These early governance decisions are critical because they ensure that security is not treated as a one-time project but as a **continuous management system** integrated into the organization's daily operations.

Equally important, the foundation phase establishes the **organizational context**—a comprehensive understanding of the internal and external factors that influence information security. This includes assessing the company's size, culture, legal obligations, stakeholder expectations, and risk appetite. For example, a financial institution operating under strict regulatory frameworks must design an ISMS that satisfies compliance mandates and audit requirements, while a technology startup may prioritize agility, innovation, and data privacy for its clients. By aligning the ISMS with the organization's real-world context, ISO 27001 becomes not only compliant but also **strategically relevant**.

The foundation phase also emphasizes **leadership involvement and cultural alignment**. Top management must demonstrate visible commitment by setting clear policies, providing adequate resources, and promoting awareness throughout the organization. Their role is not limited to approval or oversight—they must champion the ISMS as part of the organization's strategic vision. When employees see leaders prioritizing security, they are more likely to adopt responsible behaviors and internalize the importance of safeguarding information. Over time, this creates a **security-conscious culture** where everyone—from front-line staff to executives—understands their role in maintaining compliance and protecting data assets.

Moreover, this phase establishes the **risk management framework** that underpins ISO 27001. Organizations begin to identify potential threats, evaluate vulnerabilities, and set criteria for acceptable risk levels. These early assessments form the basis for selecting appropriate controls and designing mitigation strategies. By addressing these elements during the foundation stage, organizations avoid common pitfalls such as reactive decision-making or fragmented implementation.

In essence, the foundation phase is the **architectural blueprint** of the ISMS. Just as a building depends on the strength of its foundation, the effectiveness of the ISMS depends on the clarity, precision, and foresight applied at this stage. A well-defined foundation ensures that later phases—such as implementation, monitoring, and continual improvement—are built on stable ground. When approached strategically, this phase transforms ISO 27001 from a compliance requirement into a **strategic management tool** that enhances resilience, strengthens reputation, and positions the organization for sustainable growth in an increasingly digital and risk-driven world.

Initial Planning and Preparation

The **implementation journey** of ISO 27001 begins not with technology, but with **strategic planning and organizational clarity**. This early stage is where intentions become actionable goals, and high-level commitment translates into a structured roadmap. At its core, ISO 27001 implementation is a management initiative—one that requires vision, coordination, and persistence. Without a deliberate and methodical approach, even well-intentioned efforts risk becoming fragmented or losing momentum.

The process begins with **senior management defining clear objectives** for adopting ISO 27001. This clarity of purpose is essential because it determines how success will be measured and how priorities will be set. Organizations may pursue certification for various reasons—some seek to **strengthen legal and regulatory compliance**, others aim to **protect valuable intellectual property**, while many view ISO 27001 as a way to **build client confidence and improve market reputation**. Clearly articulating these motivations aligns internal teams, ensures resource allocation is justified, and provides a strategic narrative that sustains commitment throughout the implementation.

Once objectives are established, management must develop a **comprehensive implementation roadmap**. This roadmap should outline each major phase of the journey—from initial gap assessment and risk evaluation to control implementation, internal audits, and final certification review. Every phase must be backed by **defined deliverables, realistic timelines, and assigned responsibilities**. This structured approach transforms ISO 27001 from an abstract goal into a practical project plan that guides daily actions.

A well-designed roadmap also ensures **balance and coordination**. Implementing ISO 27001 involves numerous stakeholders, including IT teams, HR, legal departments, and senior executives. Without a central plan, organizations risk duplication of effort or gaps in accountability. The roadmap must therefore specify not only what will be done, but who will do it, how progress will be tracked, and how outcomes will be validated. This clarity prevents overextension of teams, minimizes delays, and ensures that critical compliance milestones are not missed.

Effective planning also includes a **thorough evaluation of the current security landscape**. Organizations should begin by reviewing existing **policies, processes, and technologies** to assess their alignment with ISO 27001 requirements. This may involve examining how information is classified, how incidents are managed, and how risks are documented and communicated. Many organizations choose to conduct a **pre-assessment or gap analysis**—a diagnostic review that compares the current state of information security against ISO 27001's clauses and controls.

A gap analysis is not merely an audit; it is a **strategic diagnostic tool**. It provides a factual understanding of the organization's maturity, identifies areas that meet compliance expectations, and highlights those requiring improvement. For example, a company may discover that while it already maintains strong technical controls (like encryption and firewalls), it lacks formal documentation, incident reporting mechanisms, or leadership oversight—elements that are equally critical for certification.

The results of the gap analysis become the **blueprint for implementation**, guiding decision-making and prioritization. By knowing precisely where weaknesses exist, organizations can focus resources efficiently and avoid unnecessary duplication of controls. It also helps in building realistic budgets and timelines, ensuring that each stage of the project is supported by the required expertise, tools, and governance.

Defining the Scope of the ISMS

Defining the **scope of the Information Security Management System (ISMS)** is one of the most critical early steps in the ISO 27001 implementation process. It serves as the foundation upon which all subsequent activities—risk assessment, control selection, audits, and continuous improvement—are built. A **precisely defined scope** ensures that the organization remains focused, efficient, and aligned with its real-world needs. Without a clear scope, implementation efforts can easily become scattered, redundant, or unmanageable, especially in complex organizations with multiple systems and departments.

The **scope** determines the **boundaries and applicability** of the ISMS. It outlines which parts of the organization will fall under the system's protection and which areas are excluded from it. This includes specifying **departments, business units, physical locations, processes, technologies, and information assets** that are covered. For instance, a multinational organization might initially limit the ISMS to one **regional office, data center, or business unit**, allowing it to test, refine, and validate the system before scaling across the enterprise. In contrast, a small or medium-sized company may find it practical to implement ISO 27001 across its entire operation from the outset.

A **well-crafted scope statement** not only identifies what is included but also explains what is **deliberately excluded**, along with sound justifications. For example, an organization might exclude a legacy system scheduled for decommissioning or a subsidiary operating under a separate legal entity. These exclusions must be logical, transparent, and defensible, as auditors will evaluate whether the defined scope truly reflects the organization's risk environment. Ambiguous or unjustified exclusions often raise questions during certification audits and can delay approval.

The scope should always align with the organization's **risk appetite, business priorities, and strategic objectives**. If an organization's main concern is protecting customer data, its ISMS scope should prioritize systems, applications, and processes where that data resides. Similarly, a company operating in a heavily regulated sector—such as finance, healthcare, or defense—should align its scope with the **regulatory frameworks** and compliance obligations relevant to those domains. This strategic alignment ensures that information security becomes an enabler of business success rather than a standalone compliance exercise.

Another key consideration is **clarity and measurability**. A vague or overly broad scope creates confusion about accountability and makes it difficult to evaluate effectiveness. Conversely, a scope that is too narrow might exclude essential processes or assets, leaving critical risks unmanaged. Therefore, the scope definition process requires **collaboration across departments**, including IT, operations, legal, and executive management, to ensure all relevant perspectives are captured. This collaborative approach not only improves accuracy but also fosters a sense of ownership across the organization.

The **scope statement** should be formally documented and approved by top management. It typically includes:

- A clear description of the ISMS boundaries (organizational, geographical, and technological).

- A list of included and excluded areas, with explanations.
- References to supporting standards, frameworks, or systems.
- Alignment with strategic goals, legal requirements, and risk considerations.

During certification, auditors use the scope statement as a **reference framework** to assess whether the ISMS meets ISO 27001 requirements within the defined limits. A well-defined scope thus simplifies audits by providing **clear evaluation parameters**, avoiding misunderstandings, and ensuring that compliance can be demonstrated with precision.

In practice, scope definition is not a one-time activity. As organizations grow, adopt new technologies, or expand operations, the scope should be **periodically reviewed and updated**. This ensures that the ISMS remains current and continues to cover all relevant areas of risk exposure. Neglecting to revise the scope when significant changes occur—such as mergers, system upgrades, or new product launches—can leave gaps in protection and undermine certification validity.

In conclusion, **defining the ISMS scope** is not a procedural formality but a **strategic exercise in focus and prioritization**. It bridges the gap between organizational objectives and security implementation, ensuring that every control, policy, and audit is grounded in real operational relevance. When done thoughtfully, scope definition sets the tone for an effective, scalable, and auditable ISMS—one that supports the organization's mission while maintaining resilience against evolving security threats.

Establishing Roles and Responsibilities

No management system can succeed without accountability. Establishing roles and responsibilities ensures that everyone involved understands their contribution to information security.

The organization should appoint an **Information Security Manager** or **ISMS Coordinator** responsible for day-to-day management and reporting. Senior management, meanwhile, must oversee policy approval, risk acceptance, and performance reviews. Departments such as IT, Human Resources, and Compliance should have designated representatives to handle specialized tasks like access control, staff training, and incident response.

Equally important is awareness among all employees. Every individual, from executives to frontline staff, plays a role in maintaining security by following procedures, reporting anomalies, and safeguarding information assets. When accountability is clearly defined, the ISMS operates as a coordinated system rather than a collection of isolated efforts.

Conducting a Risk Assessment

Risk assessment serves as the **analytical core** of ISO 27001 implementation, forming the bridge between strategy and execution. It is not simply a checklist activity, but a disciplined process of understanding uncertainty and translating it into informed decisions. At its essence, risk assessment answers three fundamental questions: *What could go wrong? How likely is it to happen? And what would be the impact if it did?* By addressing these questions systematically, organizations gain a clear, data-driven picture of their vulnerabilities and can allocate their security investments with precision.

The process begins with **identifying potential threats and vulnerabilities** that could compromise the confidentiality, integrity, or availability of information. Threats may stem from multiple sources—cyberattacks, human error, natural disasters, system failures, or even insider misuse. Vulnerabilities, in contrast, represent the internal weaknesses that allow these threats to succeed—such as outdated software, poor access controls, or lack of staff awareness. This combination of external and internal factors defines the organization's exposure to risk.

Once threats and vulnerabilities are identified, the next step is to **evaluate their likelihood and potential impact**. ISO 27001 encourages organizations to use a **structured and consistent methodology**, often based on qualitative or quantitative scoring. For example, a risk might be rated from 1 to 5 on both likelihood and impact, allowing decision-makers to visualize which risks pose the greatest concern. This assessment transforms abstract concerns into measurable values, helping leaders prioritize which issues demand immediate attention and which can be monitored over time.

The outcome of this stage is a **risk register**—a central document that captures each identified risk, its cause, potential consequences, and current mitigation measures. This register becomes the foundation for the **risk treatment plan**, which outlines the specific actions needed to reduce each risk to an acceptable level. These actions might involve implementing technical controls (like encryption or intrusion detection systems), administrative measures (like policy updates or training programs), or physical safeguards (such as access restrictions or surveillance).

A key strength of ISO 27001's approach lies in its **flexibility and proportionality**. Risk treatment is not about eliminating every possible threat—an impossible and wasteful goal—but about aligning the level of control with the **organization's risk appetite and business priorities**. For instance, a bank may accept minimal tolerance for data breaches but greater tolerance for minor operational disruptions. A research institution, on the other hand, may prioritize protecting intellectual property over day-to-day service availability. This context-driven approach ensures that every control implemented has a clear business justification.

Effective risk assessment also enables **informed resource allocation**. By quantifying and ranking risks, organizations can channel their limited budgets and personnel toward the most critical vulnerabilities, achieving maximum security value with minimal waste. This prioritization also strengthens communication with senior management, as risk results can be presented in clear, business-oriented terms rather than technical jargon. Decision-makers can then understand not just *where* risks exist, but *why* certain investments are necessary and *what impact* they will have.

Moreover, risk assessment is not a one-time task. It is a **living process** that must evolve alongside the organization's systems, technologies, and external environment. As new products are launched, vendors are added, or regulations change, the risk landscape shifts accordingly. Regularly revisiting and updating the risk assessment ensures that the Information Security Management System (ISMS) remains relevant, resilient, and responsive to emerging threats.

Identifying Potential Threats and Vulnerabilities

Every organization faces a unique set of risks shaped by its industry, size, and technological environment. The first task in risk assessment is to **identify potential threats**—events or actions that could harm the confidentiality, integrity, or availability of information. These may include cyberattacks, system failures, insider misuse, supply-chain weaknesses, or natural disasters.

At the same time, **vulnerabilities** must be examined—weaknesses that make those threats more likely to succeed. Examples include unpatched software, inadequate access controls, or insufficient employee training. By mapping threats to vulnerabilities, organizations create a realistic picture of where they are most exposed.

This stage should involve collaboration between departments, as security risks often span technical, human, and procedural areas. Workshops, interviews, and document reviews are common methods for gathering input. The goal is comprehensive awareness—not just of IT systems but of every process handling valuable information.

Assessing Impact and Likelihood

Once risks are identified, they must be analyzed in terms of **impact** and **likelihood**.

- *Impact* measures the potential damage if the event occurs, such as financial loss, reputational harm, or regulatory penalties.
- *Likelihood* estimates the probability of occurrence based on existing controls and threat activity.

Each risk is then assigned a numerical or qualitative score derived from multiplying impact and likelihood. This **risk matrix** helps prioritize actions: high-impact, high-likelihood risks demand immediate mitigation, while low-impact, low-likelihood risks may simply be monitored.

This structured evaluation promotes objective decision-making. Instead of reacting to every possible danger, the organization focuses on those risks that pose the greatest threat to its mission and stakeholders. The results form the foundation for the next phase—risk treatment and control selection.

Implementing Risk Treatment Plans

Once risks have been identified and analyzed, the next logical step is to **implement risk treatment plans**. This stage turns assessment findings into concrete, measurable actions. Each identified risk should be assigned a specific strategy, timeline, and responsible owner to ensure accountability.

A **Risk Treatment Plan** outlines how selected controls will be applied to reduce risks to acceptable levels. Controls may include technical measures—such as multi-factor authentication, encryption, or intrusion detection systems—as well as administrative and procedural actions like training programs, vendor evaluations, or policy updates.

Successful implementation depends on prioritization. High-impact and high-likelihood risks must be addressed first, with clear deadlines and resources allocated. Each control should have defined success criteria so its effectiveness can later be verified during internal audits or management reviews.

Periodic evaluation is also essential. Even well-designed controls may lose effectiveness as technologies, threats, or business operations evolve. By continuously reviewing and updating risk treatment plans, organizations ensure that their security posture remains dynamic, not static.

Ultimately, the purpose of risk treatment is not perfection but **balance**—achieving an acceptable level of protection that aligns with the organization's strategic goals and operational realities.

Developing Policies and Procedures

Key Policies Needed for Compliance

Policies and procedures form the backbone of any Information Security Management System. They translate the abstract requirements of ISO 27001 into clear expectations and repeatable actions across the organization. Each policy establishes boundaries for acceptable behavior, ensures consistency, and provides guidance for decision-making.

Typical policies required for ISO 27001 compliance include:

- **Information Security Policy:** Defines the organization's overall commitment to protecting information assets.
- **Access Control Policy:** Regulates who can access systems and data, and under what conditions.
- **Asset Management Policy:** Ensures that all assets—hardware, software, and information—are properly inventoried and classified.
- **Cryptographic Policy:** Outlines the use of encryption and key-management practices.
- **Incident Management Policy:** Specifies how to report, investigate, and resolve security incidents.
- **Business Continuity and Backup Policy:** Describes how the organization will maintain critical operations in the event of disruption.

While ISO 27001 does not prescribe the exact format of these policies, they must be documented, approved by management, communicated to relevant personnel, and regularly reviewed. Each policy should clearly state its purpose, scope, responsibilities, and consequences for non-compliance.

Creating Security Protocols and Documentation

Policies are supported by **procedures and protocols**—the detailed, step-by-step instructions that guide implementation. For instance, a policy may require that all employees use complex passwords, while the supporting procedure specifies password length, renewal frequency, and enforcement mechanisms.

Documentation serves several critical functions. It provides evidence of compliance, supports training, and ensures continuity when staff change roles. ISO 27001 requires certain types of documented information, such as the Statement of Applicability (which lists implemented controls), risk assessment results, and audit reports.

To maintain clarity, documents should follow consistent templates and version-control practices. They must be stored securely but remain easily accessible to authorized users. Proper documentation transforms information security from verbal promises into verifiable, auditable practices.

Engaging Employees and Raising Awareness

Even the most advanced controls cannot succeed without informed and engaged employees. People are both the strongest and weakest link in information security, which is why ISO 27001 emphasizes awareness and participation at every level.

Engagement begins with **education**. Employees must understand why information security matters—not only for compliance but for the organization's survival and reputation. Awareness programs should cover practical topics such as recognizing phishing emails, handling confidential data, managing passwords, and reporting suspicious activity. Regular workshops, brief reminders, and interactive e-learning modules help reinforce these principles.

Leadership plays a central role here as well. When executives actively support training initiatives and model secure behavior, employees follow their example. Creating a culture where security is viewed as a shared responsibility rather than a technical burden encourages cooperation and accountability.

Recognition and feedback mechanisms also strengthen engagement. Highlighting teams that follow best practices or promptly report incidents can motivate others to adopt similar behavior.

Finally, awareness should be continuous, not a one-time exercise. As new technologies and threats emerge, training content must evolve accordingly. Regular communication—through newsletters, dashboards, or intranet updates—keeps security top of mind and integrates it into daily work routines.

An informed workforce is the most powerful defense an organization can possess. By empowering employees to act as active participants rather than passive observers, the organization transforms ISO 27001 from a management requirement into a living culture of vigilance and responsibility.

Employee Training Programs

Training is one of the most powerful instruments for strengthening information security. ISO 27001 emphasizes that every employee — regardless of their department or rank — must understand their role in protecting organizational assets. A well-structured training program ensures that employees can identify potential risks, follow established policies, and act decisively when security incidents occur.

An effective program should start with an **initial induction session** for all new staff members, introducing the organization's ISMS objectives, data-handling procedures, and reporting mechanisms. This should be followed by **periodic refresher sessions** that reflect evolving threats, such as phishing techniques or social engineering attacks. Specialized training should also be provided for employees managing sensitive data, IT infrastructure, or customer information.

The content of each training session must be practical, engaging, and relevant to employees' daily work. Simulations, case studies, and scenario-based exercises are often more effective than lengthy theoretical presentations. Most importantly, training results should be documented and reviewed regularly to confirm that learning outcomes are achieved and sustained.

Building a Security-Conscious Culture

Policies, procedures, and technologies form the technical backbone of information security, but they cannot alone guarantee protection. The real strength of an Information Security Management System (ISMS) lies in cultivating a **security-conscious culture**, where awareness and responsibility become part of the organization's collective mindset. In such an environment, security is not perceived as an external rule imposed by management but as an instinctive part of everyday decision-making. Employees understand that protecting data is not the job of one department—it is a shared obligation that supports the organization's reputation, resilience, and trustworthiness.

A truly **security-aware workforce** behaves proactively. Staff members lock their screens when leaving workstations, verify suspicious emails before clicking, and question unusual requests rather than complying blindly. They report anomalies, incidents, or potential breaches promptly and without fear of punishment. This behavioral alignment cannot be achieved by policy alone; it requires an ongoing cultural transformation where every employee sees themselves as a **guardian of information integrity**.

The **role of leadership** is pivotal in shaping and sustaining this culture. Executives and senior managers must **set the tone from the top**, demonstrating visible commitment to information security. When leadership consistently models responsible behavior—such as following password policies, attending awareness sessions, and discussing security in strategic meetings—it signals to the entire workforce that security is not optional, but a core organizational value. Leadership's consistent messaging should frame security not as a cost or a burden, but as an enabler of trust, innovation, and competitive advantage.

Building this culture requires **strategic communication and engagement**. One-off training sessions are rarely effective; instead, organizations should employ a mix of communication tools to keep security awareness alive. Regular awareness campaigns, internal newsletters, short videos, or posters highlighting common threats such as phishing or social engineering can make security relatable and memorable. Recognizing and rewarding employees who demonstrate responsible behavior—such as promptly reporting an incident or improving a process—reinforces positive habits and shows that security is valued at every level.

Additionally, the organization should promote **psychological safety**—an atmosphere where employees feel comfortable admitting mistakes or raising concerns without fear of blame. In traditional work environments, employees often hide security lapses out of fear of disciplinary action, which can delay response and exacerbate damage. A mature organization encourages openness: if someone accidentally shares sensitive information or suspects a phishing attempt, they should be confident that reporting it promptly will lead to resolution, not reprimand. This trust-based environment transforms security reporting from a reactive obligation into a **collaborative process of continuous improvement**.

A sustainable security culture also depends on **clear accountability and empowerment**. Employees at all levels should understand the security expectations associated with their roles. Job descriptions, onboarding programs, and performance reviews can incorporate security responsibilities, ensuring that vigilance becomes a measurable and rewarded behavior. At the same time, employees must be equipped with the **knowledge and tools** to act securely—whether that means understanding how to classify documents, manage passwords, or detect social engineering tactics.

As the culture matures, security awareness evolves from routine compliance into **organizational instinct**. Teams begin to anticipate risks rather than merely reacting to them. Collaboration between departments strengthens, as IT, HR, and operations align around shared goals of resilience and trust. Over time, security ceases to be viewed as a barrier to productivity and instead becomes a natural component of efficient, ethical, and professional business practice.

Internal Audits and Self-Assessment

How to Conduct Internal Audits Effectively

Internal audits are the backbone of continuous improvement under ISO 27001. They provide a structured opportunity to evaluate whether policies, procedures, and controls are functioning as intended. The objective is not to assign blame but to identify gaps, verify effectiveness, and strengthen the ISMS.

An internal audit begins with an **audit plan** that defines the scope, criteria, and schedule. Auditors should be impartial and ideally independent from the departments being audited. During the audit, they collect evidence through document reviews, interviews, and observations. Findings are then categorized as conformities, nonconformities, or opportunities for improvement.

Effective auditors focus on both compliance and performance. They not only confirm whether controls are implemented but also assess whether those controls achieve their intended results. The audit report should clearly outline findings, recommended corrective actions, and timelines for completion.

Preparing for External Audits

An external audit, conducted by an accredited certification body, validates the organization's compliance with ISO 27001. Preparation begins long before the audit date. Documentation should be current, controls tested, and all corrective actions from previous internal audits resolved.

Employees must be briefed on their roles and ready to demonstrate awareness of relevant policies. Management should ensure that the Statement of Applicability, risk assessments, and treatment plans are accurate and up to date.

During the external audit, transparency and cooperation are key. Auditors look for evidence of consistent practice, not perfection. Demonstrating commitment to continuous improvement often makes a stronger impression than striving for a flawless record.

Successfully completing an external audit not only earns certification but also reinforces credibility with clients, regulators, and stakeholders, proving that the organization takes information security seriously.

Establishing Metrics for Success

Measurement is the foundation of continual improvement. ISO 27001 requires organizations to define **Key Performance Indicators (KPIs)** that track the effectiveness of their ISMS. These metrics provide visibility into whether controls are working and whether objectives are being met.

Common examples include the number of detected security incidents, time taken to resolve them, compliance rates in employee training, frequency of system patching, and audit results. Metrics should be specific, measurable, and linked to the organization's overall strategic goals.

Regularly reviewing these metrics helps management make informed decisions. If certain indicators show declining performance — for example, an increase in phishing incidents or delays in incident response — corrective actions can be initiated immediately.

By establishing clear metrics, organizations can demonstrate progress, justify investments, and maintain accountability. Effective measurement transforms ISO 27001 from a static compliance exercise into a dynamic system of performance management and continuous learning.

Professional Fillable Templates

Template 1: Employee Training and Awareness Tracker

Category	Purpose / Explanation	To Be Filled by Organization
Training Type	Specify the type of training conducted (e.g., Awareness, Technical, Incident Response).	________________________
Target Audience	Define the group receiving the training (e.g., All Staff, IT Team, HR Department).	________________________
Completion & Evaluation	Indicate completion date and summarize participant feedback or assessment results.	________________________

Template 2: Internal Audit and KPI Monitoring Sheet

Metric / Area	Objective / Measurement Criteria	Results / Follow-up Actions
Audit Finding / KPI	Describe the control or performance metric being monitored.	________________________
Performance Target	Define expected level or compliance goal.	________________________

Corrective / Preventive Action	Record planned improvements and assigned responsibilities.	______________________________

Defining KPIs to Track Progress

Key Performance Indicators (KPIs) are essential tools for measuring the success and maturity of an organization's Information Security Management System (ISMS). They provide quantifiable evidence of how effectively security objectives are being met and help identify areas that require improvement.

In the context of ISO 27001, KPIs bridge the gap between policy and performance. While policies define *what* must be achieved, KPIs show *how well* those goals are being realized. They offer management a factual basis for decision-making, ensuring that resources are directed toward areas of genuine need rather than assumptions.

When defining KPIs, organizations should align them with both **business objectives** and **risk management outcomes**. Each indicator should be specific, measurable, achievable, relevant, and time-bound (SMART). Vague or overly broad metrics often lead to confusion or misinterpretation.

Examples of effective KPIs for an ISMS include:

- Number of security incidents detected and resolved within a defined time frame
- Percentage of employees completing security awareness training
- Average response time to reported vulnerabilities or breaches
- Frequency of system patching and updates
- Compliance rate with data backup and recovery procedures
- Number of audit nonconformities closed within target dates

It is also important to balance **quantitative** and **qualitative** indicators. Quantitative data—such as incident frequency—provides measurable trends, while qualitative insights—such as employee feedback on training effectiveness—add context to those results.

The process of defining KPIs should involve multiple stakeholders, including management, IT, compliance officers, and risk owners. This collaboration ensures that metrics are both meaningful and achievable within existing operational constraints.

Ultimately, KPIs turn information security into a continuous feedback loop. They provide visibility, accountability, and the ability to demonstrate tangible progress toward maintaining confidentiality, integrity, and availability across all information assets.

Reporting and Continuous Improvement

Once KPIs are defined, their true value emerges through consistent **monitoring and reporting**. ISO 27001 emphasizes that performance data must be regularly analyzed, communicated, and acted upon. Reports should not be static documents but living tools that inform decision-making and drive improvement.

Performance reporting begins with collecting KPI data from various sources such as incident logs, audit results, risk registers, and employee training systems. This data should be compiled into concise, visual reports—often using dashboards or scorecards—that allow leadership to quickly understand trends and anomalies.

Regular reporting to top management is vital. These sessions should focus not only on compliance status but also on effectiveness: whether implemented controls are achieving their intended purpose. Management reviews, typically conducted at planned intervals, are a formal requirement under ISO 27001 and serve as the cornerstone of continuous improvement.

During these reviews, management evaluates:

- Achievement of ISMS objectives and targets
- Audit findings and corrective actions

- Effectiveness of risk treatments and controls
- Opportunities for process enhancement
- Changes in internal or external factors that may affect the ISMS

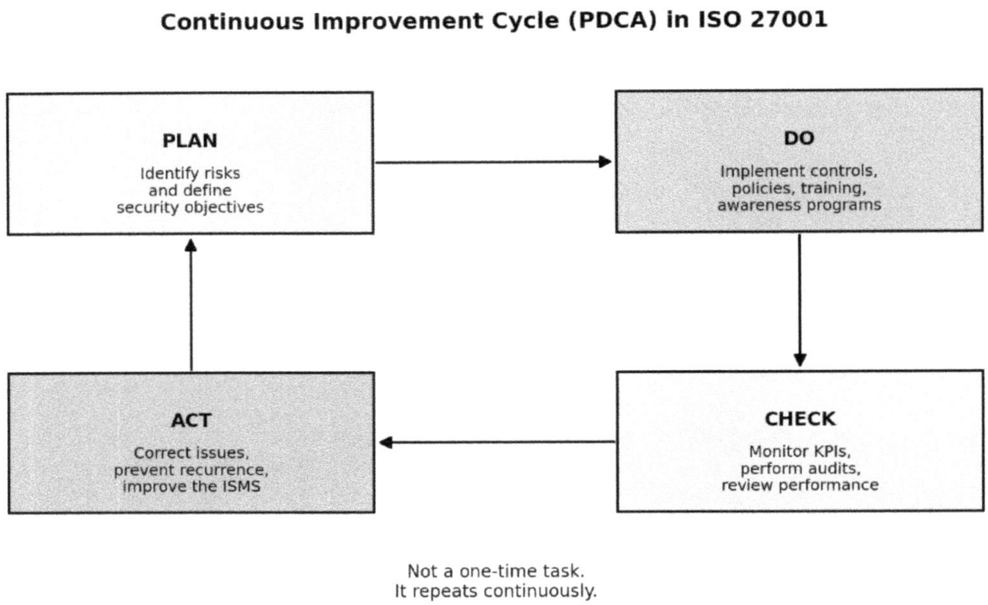

The outcome of these reviews should include **decisions and actions** related to resource allocation, policy updates, training enhancements, or technology investments. Each improvement action must be tracked to completion and reassessed for effectiveness.

Continuous improvement, in this context, is not a one-time event but an ongoing cycle of **Plan–Do–Check–Act (PDCA)**.

- **Plan:** Identify risks and define objectives.
- **Do:** Implement policies, controls, and awareness programs.
- **Check:** Measure performance through KPIs and audits.
- **Act:** Apply corrective and preventive actions to enhance results.

Over time, this cycle cultivates resilience and adaptability. As new technologies, threats, and regulations emerge, the ISMS evolves with them—ensuring that information security remains aligned with organizational growth and external expectations.

In essence, effective reporting and improvement transform ISO 27001 from a compliance framework into a strategic management system. It empowers leaders to make evidence-based decisions, fosters accountability across departments, and reinforces a culture where security excellence becomes a continuous pursuit rather than a final destination.

Conclusion

Implementing ISO 27001 is far more than a compliance exercise; it is a strategic transformation that integrates information security into the very fabric of an organization. This chapter has demonstrated that success lies in following a structured, disciplined approach — from careful planning and risk assessment to employee engagement and measurable performance tracking.

The journey begins with defining the ISMS scope, understanding risks, and creating treatment plans that balance protection with practicality. Leadership plays a decisive role in shaping direction, setting expectations, and ensuring that security objectives are aligned with overall business goals. Without visible executive commitment, even the most sophisticated frameworks fail to gain traction.

Equally vital is the human element. Employees are not simply subjects of policy — they are active participants in safeguarding organizational assets. Training, awareness, and consistent communication cultivate a security-conscious culture that complements technological controls and policy frameworks.

Internal audits, self-assessments, and continuous reporting form the backbone of accountability. Through clearly defined KPIs and structured management reviews, organizations can measure what truly matters — performance, progress, and resilience. The resulting insights fuel continuous improvement, ensuring that the ISMS evolves alongside new threats, technologies, and regulations.

In essence, ISO 27001 implementation is an ongoing commitment rather than a one-time project. It demands foresight, discipline, and collaboration across all levels of the organization. When executed effectively, it not only strengthens defenses against cyber threats but also builds credibility, trust, and long-term sustainability. The foundation laid in this chapter prepares the organization to move confidently toward the next stage — **achieving certification and maintaining enduring compliance**, which will be explored in Chapter 4.

CHAPTER 4:

Maintaining and Monitoring Your ISMS

Ongoing Risk Management

A strong ISMS does not stand still. Threats evolve, technologies change, and business models shift. Ongoing risk management keeps your controls aligned with reality and ensures that protection remains proportional to exposure.

How to stay ahead of emerging threats

Start with structured threat intelligence. Track reputable advisories, vendor bulletins, sector ISAC updates, and vulnerability feeds. Translate external signals into internal actions by mapping each new threat to your assets, data flows, and suppliers. Treat threat watching as a weekly operational task, not an occasional research effort. Assign clear ownership for collection, triage, and escalation so that signals do not get lost.

Harden your environment through continuous control care. Keep configuration baselines current. Patch with defined service level targets, tested rollback plans, and exception logs for systems that cannot be updated immediately. For cloud workloads, apply policy-as-code to enforce guardrails at scale. For identity, close privilege creep through quarterly access reviews, strong authentication, and conditional access rules.

Exercise your incident response muscle. Run tabletop drills and technical simulations that test detection, escalation, and communication. Each rehearsal should end with lessons learned, ticketed follow-ups, and owners. Repetition builds confidence and shortens response times.

Regular risk reviews and updates

Set a risk review cadence that matches your change rate. Many organizations review key risks quarterly and perform a fuller reassessment annually, with ad hoc updates when major changes occur, such as a merger, a new product, or a critical supplier onboarded. Use a consistent method for scoring likelihood and impact so that trends are meaningful over time.

Update the risk register when controls change, when new vulnerabilities are found, or when the business context shifts. Recalculate residual risk and confirm that acceptance decisions still hold. If not, issue a change to the Risk Treatment Plan with dates, budgets, and owners. Close the loop in management reviews so leadership can approve risk acceptance or require further treatment.

Internal Audits and Monitoring

Audits and operational monitoring are the feedback mechanisms of the ISMS. Together they reveal what is working, what is drifting, and what needs improvement.

Best practices for auditing your ISMS

Plan with purpose. Define the audit scope from real risks and past findings, not only from a checklist. Keep auditors independent from the areas they review. Publish an audit plan that lists objectives, criteria, evidence sources, and timelines so auditees can prepare.

Collect evidence that is observable, repeatable, and time-bound. Favor samples drawn from recent periods. Trace each sample from policy to procedure to record so that you test both design and operation. When you find an issue, write it as a clear nonconformity with the requirement cited, the gap observed, and the risk it creates. Recommend corrective action that is practical and measurable.

Close findings with discipline. Use root cause analysis to avoid superficial fixes. Assign owners, due dates, and success criteria. Verify effectiveness after completion, not only completion itself. Summarize outcomes in the management review so decisions and resources follow the evidence.

Operational monitoring that complements audits

Build dashboards that track leading and lagging indicators. Leading indicators include patch currency, backup verification rates, mean time to detect, and phishing simulation results. Lagging indicators include confirmed incidents, downtime, and audit nonconformities. Automate collection where possible so reports are timely and trusted. When a metric trends in the wrong direction, open an improvement action and assign ownership. Monitoring without action does not create value.

Fillable Templates

Template 1: Quarterly Risk Review Sheet

Section	Purpose	To Complete

Top Risks This Quarter	List the three highest residual risks with brief rationale.	1) __________ 2) __________ 3) __________
Changes Since Last Review	Note new threats, assets, suppliers, or regulatory drivers.	__________
Treatment Updates	Actions added or revised, with dates and owners.	Action: __________ Owner: __________ Target Date: __________

Template 2: Internal Audit and Monitoring Tracker

Section	Purpose	To Complete
Audit Scope & Criteria	Area audited, clauses or controls tested, time window.	Scope:__________ Criteria: __________ Period: __________
Key Findings & Risk	Summarize conformities, nonconformities, and associated risk.	Finding: __________ Risk: __________
Corrective Action & Verification	Planned fix, owner, deadline, and post-fix verification result.	Action: __________ Owner: __________ Due: __________ Verified On: __________

Maintaining Audit Readiness

Audit readiness is not a final checkpoint before certification; it is a continuous state of preparedness. A well-maintained ISMS should always be ready to demonstrate its effectiveness, with evidence organized and accessible at any moment.

Maintaining readiness begins with a clear audit calendar that outlines regular internal audits, management reviews, and risk assessments. When these activities are scheduled consistently, the organization avoids last-minute stress and ensures that findings are resolved in real time rather than accumulated for year-end.

Equally important is maintaining current and traceable evidence. Every implemented control should have supporting documentation—policies, logs, training records, incident reports, access reviews, and test results. Each record must clearly indicate what was done, when it was done, and by whom. This transparency shows auditors that controls operate as intended and that accountability is built into daily routines.

A clean, updated **Statement of Applicability** is also vital. It should accurately reflect which controls are in place, which have been excluded, and why. Whenever risks, assets, or processes change, the SoA should be reviewed and updated accordingly.

Mock audits are an effective way to sustain readiness. By simulating real audit conditions, organizations can identify weak points, measure response time, and train staff to communicate confidently and clearly. The goal is not perfection but familiarity—when employees understand their roles and can discuss procedures naturally, audit sessions become collaborative rather than stressful.

Continuous Improvement and Adaptation

The Importance of Feedback Loops

A successful ISMS thrives on learning. Feedback loops connect operational reality with strategic oversight, allowing the organization to correct course before problems escalate. These loops collect information from multiple sources—incident investigations, KPI reports, internal audits, threat intelligence, and employee feedback—and translate it into measurable improvements.

Each feedback channel feeds into a unified improvement process where findings are documented, actions assigned, and effectiveness verified. This cycle ensures that lessons are not only recorded but acted upon. When feedback loops are strong, the ISMS becomes adaptive, evolving naturally with new technologies, threats, and business priorities.

How to Improve Security Controls Over Time

Improvement begins with clarity. Each control should have a defined purpose and measurable success indicators. Regular assessments help determine whether a control still serves its intended goal or whether it has become outdated. If incidents occur, the response should go beyond fixing immediate symptoms to addressing underlying causes—such as process gaps, unclear roles, or lack of training.

Introducing changes gradually allows testing and validation before full deployment. Pilot programs, limited rollouts, and controlled experiments reduce risk and provide data for informed decisions. Over time, repetitive or well-defined processes can be automated to enhance efficiency and accuracy.

Improvement also includes letting go of obsolete practices. When a control no longer adds value or when newer technology provides better protection, retiring the old measure keeps the ISMS lean and relevant. Regular reassessment ensures that the security framework grows in alignment with organizational goals rather than becoming a bureaucratic burden.

Continuous improvement, at its core, transforms the ISMS from a compliance structure into a living management system—resilient, responsive, and committed to excellence.

Documentation and Record Keeping

Documentation is the backbone of an effective ISMS. It demonstrates accountability, preserves knowledge, and provides the evidence needed for both audits and decision-making. Proper record keeping ensures that every element of the system—policies, procedures, risk assessments, incident reports, and corrective actions—is clearly traceable.

Each document should be complete, authentic, dated, and attributed to a responsible person or system. Maintaining version control prevents confusion and ensures that only approved documents are used. Superseded versions should be archived securely for reference, preserving a transparent record of change.

Records must be organized logically and stored in a secure but accessible repository. The structure should mirror the ISMS framework—grouped by clauses, controls, or processes—so that information can be retrieved quickly during an audit or review. Well-indexed repositories demonstrate control and confidence to auditors.

Retention policies should reflect legal, contractual, and business requirements. Sensitive documents require strict access controls, encryption where appropriate, and regular backup testing to ensure recoverability. Documentation should integrate with daily workflows rather than exist as a separate administrative burden. When evidence is produced automatically through normal operations—such as tickets, logs, or automated reports—it remains both reliable and easy to maintain.

Ensuring Proper Documentation for Audits

Proper documentation is the foundation of a transparent and credible audit process. During an ISO 27001 audit, every claim of compliance must be supported by evidence, and that evidence must be accurate, organized, and readily retrievable. Good documentation does not just satisfy auditors; it demonstrates that the organization's ISMS operates systematically and consistently.

An effective documentation system should clearly link each control or process to its corresponding evidence. For example, access control policies should be supported by access logs and review records; incident response procedures should align with real incident reports and post-incident reviews. This alignment between policy and practice proves that the ISMS is not theoretical—it is actively functioning.

Effectively Communicating Results to Management

Effective communication with management is one of the most critical aspects of maintaining an ISO 27001-compliant ISMS. The value of an information security program is not measured only by how many controls are implemented but by how clearly its outcomes are understood by leadership and how those outcomes influence strategic decisions.

Communication must be purposeful. Executives are responsible for allocating resources and shaping organizational direction, so they need information that connects technical activities to business objectives. Instead of overwhelming them with technical jargon or compliance minutiae, reports should present **impact, trends, and strategic relevance**.

For example, rather than stating, *"Ten vulnerabilities were patched this month,"* a more meaningful statement is, *"The risk exposure from high-severity vulnerabilities dropped by 40%, reducing the probability of service disruption in our core application."* This shift from technical count to business impact helps management appreciate the ISMS as a business enabler rather than a cost center.

Regular communication builds trust and alignment. Management reviews, quarterly briefings, and concise dashboards allow security leaders to highlight achievements, report incidents, and discuss future needs. It is also essential to maintain transparency about challenges. Communicating emerging risks, resource gaps, or recurring issues demonstrates accountability and fosters informed decision-making.

When management understands both the successes and the areas that need attention, they are more likely to support policy changes, approve investments, and champion the ISMS across departments. Clear communication ensures that leadership sees information security not as an isolated function but as an integral part of organizational resilience and reputation.

Using KPIs to Demonstrate the Value of the ISMS

Key Performance Indicators (KPIs) translate the effectiveness of the ISMS into measurable terms. They provide management with quantifiable proof that security initiatives are achieving their objectives and contributing to organizational performance. Well-designed KPIs answer three essential questions: *Are our controls working? Are we managing risk effectively? Are we improving over time?*

KPIs should be specific, relevant, and linked to business priorities. Common examples include:

- **Incident response time:** how quickly the organization detects, analyzes, and resolves security incidents.
- **Vulnerability closure rate:** percentage of identified vulnerabilities remediated within defined time frames.

- **Employee awareness participation:** number or percentage of employees completing mandatory security training.
- **Policy compliance rate:** proportion of departments or processes adhering to ISMS procedures.
- **Third-party assessment coverage:** percentage of critical vendors reviewed for security compliance.
- **Audit non-conformities resolved:** rate at which audit findings are addressed and closed.

These metrics should be visualized through simple dashboards or executive summaries that show progress over time rather than isolated snapshots. Trends—whether improving or declining—offer context and direction. For instance, a gradual decline in phishing-click rates indicates that training and awareness programs are working.

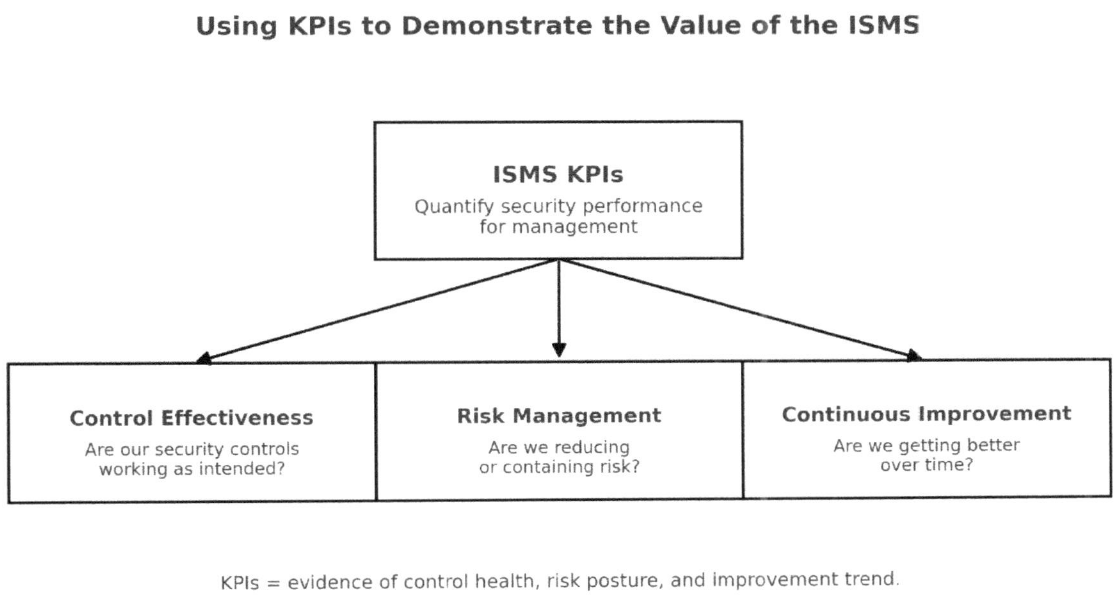

The presentation of KPIs should focus on **value, not just activity**. Management cares less about the number of logs analyzed and more about how those efforts reduce downtime, protect customer trust, and ensure compliance with laws and contracts. Each KPI should, therefore, connect back to a tangible business outcome—risk reduction, operational continuity, or reputational gain.

Finally, KPIs should evolve with the organization. As new threats, technologies, and regulations emerge, the ISMS must adapt its performance indicators accordingly. Periodic reviews of KPI relevance ensure that the metrics continue to reflect current objectives and challenges.

By consistently reporting meaningful KPIs, the ISMS establishes credibility and demonstrates its return on investment. This evidence-driven approach transforms security from a compliance requirement into a strategic advantage that supports sustainable growth and stakeholder confidence.

Documents should be version-controlled, approved by authorized personnel, and regularly reviewed to reflect current operations. Stale or outdated documents weaken audit credibility. Each file should contain essential metadata—such as author, date, version, and approval signature—so auditors can verify authenticity.

Accessibility is equally important. During an audit, being able to retrieve a document promptly reflects maturity and preparedness. Using a centralized, well-structured repository—whether a digital platform or secure intranet—ensures that all documentation follows a logical hierarchy. Files grouped by clauses or Annex A controls make cross-reference simple and efficient.

Consistent, well-maintained documentation sends a clear message: the organization is disciplined, transparent, and confident in its ISMS. It turns audit sessions into structured reviews rather than reactive searches for evidence.

Records Management Best Practices

Strong records management is what keeps documentation reliable over time. Every record—from risk assessments to training attendance sheets—serves as historical proof that the organization's ISMS decisions were deliberate and evidence-based.

Best practice begins with defining what constitutes a record within the ISMS. These may include risk registers, incident logs, asset inventories, supplier assessments, change requests, internal audit reports, or management-review minutes. Each record type should have an assigned owner responsible for maintaining accuracy and ensuring that the data remains complete.

Retention policies must specify how long each record is kept and under what conditions it can be archived or destroyed. Legal and contractual obligations often dictate minimum retention periods, but organizations should balance these requirements with storage and privacy considerations.

Records should always remain secure but accessible to authorized personnel. Using access controls, encryption, and audit trails ensures integrity and confidentiality. Regular backup testing protects against accidental loss, while encryption guards against unauthorized disclosure.

Finally, records must be integrated into the organization's daily workflow. When employees create and store evidence automatically—through ticketing systems, monitoring dashboards, or change-management tools—record keeping becomes effortless and reliable. This seamless integration ensures that the ISMS remains audit-ready at all times.

Handling Non-Conformities and Corrective Actions

No system operates flawlessly. ISO 27001 recognizes that errors, oversights, and deviations will occur. What defines a mature organization is how effectively it detects, documents, and corrects them. Handling non-conformities promptly and transparently is central to maintaining trust in the ISMS.

A **non-conformity** arises when a process or control fails to meet a requirement—whether that requirement comes from ISO 27001, internal policy, or regulatory obligations. Identifying these issues early allows for quick containment before they escalate into incidents.

Each non-conformity should be recorded with enough detail for analysis: what happened, when it occurred, which requirement was breached, and what the potential impact is. After documentation, the organization must investigate the root cause. Understanding why a failure occurred—rather than merely fixing the symptom—prevents repetition.

Once the cause is clear, a **Corrective Action Plan (CAP)** should be developed. This plan specifies what action will be taken, who is responsible, when it will be completed, and how success will be verified. Actions may include updating a procedure, retraining employees, or strengthening a control.

Corrective actions should be tracked to completion, with follow-up reviews confirming their effectiveness. If the same issue resurfaces, it indicates that the root cause was not properly addressed and further analysis is required. Documenting every step—from detection to verification—creates a transparent trail that auditors and management can review with confidence.

Over time, this structured approach turns non-conformities into opportunities for growth. Each resolved issue strengthens the ISMS, making it more resilient and reliable.

Reporting and Communicating Results

Transparent reporting is the bridge between operational performance and executive decision-making. ISO 27001 places great emphasis on communication because information security affects every level of the organization.

Reporting should transform raw data into meaningful insights. Audit results, incident analyses, risk updates, and KPI trends must be presented in a form that decision-makers can understand quickly. Clear visual dashboards, concise summaries, and trend comparisons are far more effective than dense technical reports.

Effective reporting is consistent in frequency and format. Regularly scheduled reports—monthly for operational metrics, quarterly for audits and risk, and annually for management review—create rhythm and predictability. Each report should highlight key findings, actions taken, outstanding risks, and resource needs.

Communication should also flow across all levels, not just upward. Department heads, system owners, and staff must receive relevant information about the ISMS so they can act on it. Sharing lessons learned from incidents or audits reinforces a culture of awareness and accountability.

When issues are escalated, communication must be factual, constructive, and solution-oriented. Over-reporting minor details can dilute focus, while under-reporting significant risks can cause oversight. The goal is balance: giving leadership enough insight to guide decisions without overwhelming them with noise.

External communication is equally important when required. Some organizations share summarized security metrics or audit results with customers and regulators to demonstrate transparency and compliance. Doing so responsibly builds confidence and enhances reputation.

Conclusion

Maintaining and monitoring an ISMS is not a static process but a continuous commitment to vigilance, accountability, and improvement. Once the system is implemented, its true strength lies in how effectively it adapts to change—technological, organizational, and environmental. ISO 27001 encourages organizations to treat information security as a living discipline, one that evolves through ongoing assessment and refinement.

A well-maintained ISMS thrives on regular risk reviews, timely updates, and proactive management of new threats. Internal audits, far from being routine checks, serve as valuable diagnostic tools that reveal weaknesses, measure control effectiveness, and reinforce confidence in the system's reliability. Organizations that integrate audit readiness into their daily operations are always prepared to demonstrate compliance, rather than scrambling to assemble evidence at the last moment.

Documentation and record keeping are the backbone of this process. Every policy, record, and report should provide a clear trace of accountability, ensuring that actions can be verified and improvements measured. Proper documentation transforms the ISMS from a theoretical framework into a verifiable, trustworthy structure supported by tangible proof.

Equally important is the ability to respond effectively when things go wrong. Handling non-conformities and corrective actions promptly prevents small issues from escalating into systemic failures. Each corrective action is an opportunity to strengthen resilience and refine processes for the future.

Effective communication and reporting complete the cycle. When management receives meaningful insights backed by clear KPIs, they begin to see the ISMS not as a compliance burden but as a strategic asset. Transparent communication aligns information security with business objectives, ensures sustained support from leadership, and fosters a culture of accountability throughout the organization.

Ultimately, maintaining and monitoring the ISMS is about building trust—within the organization, with partners, and with customers. It ensures that the system remains dynamic, credible, and ready to face evolving risks. The next step, explored in the following chapter, focuses on **achieving certification and sustaining long-term compliance**, where all these principles converge into measurable, certifiable success.

CHAPTER 5:

Achieving and Sustaining ISO 27001 Certification

Preparing for ISO 27001 Certification

Achieving certification is the natural outcome of a mature, well-run ISMS. Preparation is not about last-minute fixes. It is about proving that your system is designed well, operated consistently, and improved over time.

Begin by confirming that the scope of the ISMS is correct and still aligned with business priorities. The scope statement should be precise, justified, and reflected in your controls, risk register, and documentation. If the organization has grown, changed suppliers, or moved to new platforms, bring the scope up to date before engaging a certification body.

Review policies, procedures, and records against the standard's clauses and Annex A controls. The Statement of Applicability must match reality. Where a control is not applicable, the reason should be sound and recorded. Evidence should exist to show both design and operation. Policies without corresponding logs, tickets, or reports do not demonstrate effectiveness.

Assess risk management quality. Your methodology should produce consistent results. Risks need to be identified, analyzed for likelihood and impact, treated with defined controls, and tracked through to residual risk. Acceptance decisions should be approved by management and revisited at planned intervals.

Strengthen operational readiness. Ensure patching, backup verification, access reviews, incident handling, and vendor assessments are current and demonstrable. Training records should show that people know their responsibilities and have acknowledged relevant policies. Internal audits and management reviews should be recent, with findings closed or on credible plans.

Finally, conduct a realistic readiness review. A short, impartial mock audit helps validate that evidence is orderly, interviews are smooth, and retrieval is quick. Treat the results as a rehearsal for the real event, not a formality.

Understanding the Audit Process

Certification typically unfolds in two stages. The first is a documentation and readiness review that checks whether your ISMS is designed to meet requirements. The second examines how well the ISMS operates in practice.

During the stage one review, auditors evaluate the scope, policies, risk methodology, Statement of Applicability, and core procedures. They look for coherence and completeness. Gaps found here become opportunities to strengthen design before the stage two assessment.

Stage two focuses on implementation. Auditors sample evidence across departments and sites, interview personnel, and trace records from policy to procedure to proof. They look for consistency over time. Findings are categorized as conformities, nonconformities, or opportunities for improvement. Major nonconformities must be resolved before certification can be granted, while minor ones require timely corrective action.

If successful, the certification body issues a certificate with a defined validity period, subject to surveillance audits. These surveillance visits verify ongoing operation and improvement. A recertification audit occurs at the end of the cycle to renew the certificate.

Transparency and cooperation are essential throughout. Auditors expect honest answers, prompt evidence, and a clear line of ownership for processes and records. A confident, well-prepared team makes the audit constructive and efficient.

Choosing a Certification Body

Selecting the right certification body influences the credibility of your certificate and the quality of your audit experience. Look for accreditation status with a recognized national accreditation body. Accreditation proves that the certifier follows international rules and is regularly assessed for competence.

Industry experience matters. A certifier familiar with your sector understands typical risks, technologies, and regulatory pressures. This knowledge leads to relevant sampling and practical recommendations rather than generic, checkbox reviews.

Consider geographic coverage and language capability if you operate across regions. Review the certifier's availability, audit scheduling flexibility, and clarity of commercial terms. Ask about auditor qualifications, conflict-of-interest controls, and how they maintain independence when offering optional pre-assessment services.

Request sample audit plans and reporting formats. A good certification body provides a clear audit agenda, evidence expectations, and timelines for reporting and follow-up. Speak with references in similar organizations to understand responsiveness, professionalism, and the usefulness of findings.

Balance cost with value. The least expensive option is not always the best. You are choosing a long-term assurance partner who will visit regularly, challenge your system thoughtfully, and represent your certification to clients and regulators.

What to Expect from the Certification Body

A reputable certification body provides structure, clarity, and consistency. Before the audit, you should receive a formal proposal, an audit plan aligned to your scope, and information on evidence sampling and interview logistics. The plan will identify the sites and functions to be assessed and the estimated time required.

During the audit, expect professional conduct, impartiality, and evidence-based conclusions. Auditors will interview staff, inspect facilities where applicable, and examine records for completeness and timeliness. They should explain the basis for each finding and allow you to provide clarifications or additional evidence.

At the closing meeting, you will receive a clear summary of results. Nonconformities should be written in a way that cites the requirement, describes the observed gap, and explains the risk. You will also receive instructions on how to submit corrective actions and the timeframe to do so.

After certification is granted, the body will schedule surveillance audits. These are not repeats of stage two but targeted reviews of operation, previous findings, and areas of change. You can expect guidance on planning and scope for each visit, along with consistent auditors where possible to preserve continuity.

Above all, expect a relationship built on objectivity and respect. The auditor's role is to assess, not to consult, yet a strong certifier adds value by making findings precise, actionable, and grounded in the standard.

The ISO 27001 Certification Audit

The ISO 27001 certification audit is the formal stage where an independent body evaluates how effectively your organization's Information Security Management System operates. It is not intended to intimidate; rather, it validates that the organization's policies, processes, and controls work together as a coherent, well-maintained system.

The process begins with an opening meeting during which auditors confirm the scope and objectives of the audit and outline how evidence will be reviewed. They then spend time interviewing staff, examining documents, and observing day-to-day practices. Every policy or control described in the ISMS must be supported by verifiable proof that it exists in daily operation and delivers the intended results.

Throughout the assessment, auditors look for alignment between what is written and what actually happens. They may examine risk registers, incident records, access reviews, or staff training documentation to confirm that information security is consistently applied. They also check that corrective actions from earlier internal audits have been completed and that lessons learned are properly documented.

At the end of the audit, a closing meeting summarizes the findings. The auditors present a balanced view, identifying areas of conformity and highlighting any weaknesses that require correction. Major issues must be addressed before certification can be granted, while minor ones can be closed later with evidence of corrective action. The entire process is designed to provide assurance, not punishment—it demonstrates maturity, accountability, and readiness for certification.

Auditors typically concentrate on several key areas that define an effective ISMS. They assess how committed leadership is to information security and whether top management has set clear objectives that align with business strategy. They evaluate how risks are identified, analyzed, and treated in a structured manner. They examine operational controls to ensure that procedures are followed consistently and that employees understand their responsibilities. They also verify that monitoring, internal audits, and management reviews are performed regularly and used to drive improvement.

Passing the audit depends largely on preparation and confidence. When documentation is up to date and staff are comfortable discussing their roles, the process runs smoothly. Every employee should know where relevant records are kept and how they contribute to protecting information assets. It is important to communicate honestly during interviews and to demonstrate progress where full implementation is still in motion. After the audit, responding quickly to findings with realistic corrective actions confirms professionalism and strengthens trust with the auditors.

Ultimately, success in the certification audit reflects a culture of consistency. An organization that manages information security continuously, rather than rushing to prepare for the audit, naturally meets ISO 27001 requirements. The audit becomes a confirmation of strength rather than a search for faults.

Fillable Template – Audit Preparation Tracker

Audit Aspect	Evidence / Records to Present	Responsible Person & Follow-Up Action
Leadership and Commitment	Management review minutes, information security objectives, communication records	
Risk Assessment and Treatment	Updated risk register, risk treatment documentation, approvals for residual risk	

Operational Controls and Training	Access control reviews, incident reports, employee awareness training evidence	

Surveillance Audits and Maintaining Certification

Achieving ISO 27001 certification is a major accomplishment, but it is not the end of the journey. Certification marks the beginning of an ongoing commitment to maintaining and improving your Information Security Management System. Once certified, an organization enters a surveillance cycle that ensures the ISMS continues to perform effectively and evolve with changes in technology, operations, and risk.

After certification, surveillance audits are conducted by the same certification body, usually once or twice per year. These audits are shorter than the initial certification audit but equally important. They focus on confirming that the ISMS is functioning as described, that policies remain relevant, and that the organization continues to meet ISO 27001 requirements.

During a surveillance audit, auditors review records, observe operations, and check that corrective actions from previous findings have been completed. They assess whether risk assessments are updated regularly and whether management reviews are taking place as planned. Auditors also look for evidence of continual improvement—showing that lessons from incidents, new regulations, or emerging threats have been incorporated into the system.

Maintaining certification year-round depends on discipline and integration. Security processes should be woven into everyday operations rather than treated as isolated compliance exercises. Training, access management, change control, and incident response must all be part of the organization's natural rhythm. Regular internal audits, management reviews, and KPI tracking ensure that issues are detected early and corrected before they appear in a formal audit.

When an organization treats the ISMS as a living system—reviewed, tested, and improved continuously—maintaining certification becomes a routine outcome rather than a stressful event.

Demonstrating the Value of Certification

The real worth of ISO 27001 certification lies in how it strengthens organizational credibility and stakeholder confidence. Beyond demonstrating compliance, it communicates that the organization takes data protection, privacy, and business continuity seriously. This visible assurance builds trust with clients, partners, and regulators.

Maintaining certification enhances reputation and can provide a competitive advantage. Many companies now require suppliers to be certified as part of their procurement criteria. A valid ISO 27001 certificate signals maturity, responsibility, and readiness to meet contractual obligations. It can also reduce the time and complexity of external security assessments, as certification already serves as verified proof of due diligence.

Internally, certification reinforces consistency. It gives employees a structured framework for managing information security and helps align security goals with broader business objectives. It encourages collaboration across departments and establishes a shared understanding of risk.

The reputational impact extends beyond compliance. In an age where data breaches damage trust overnight, an organization that maintains ISO 27001 certification shows resilience and transparency. It demonstrates not only that the company protects information but also that it invests in continuous improvement. This perception of reliability can strengthen customer loyalty and open doors to new markets.

Handling Non-Conformities Post-Certification

Even after certification, non-conformities can occur. What distinguishes a mature organization is how quickly and effectively it responds. Non-conformities may arise from new risks, process changes, staff turnover, or simple human error. Addressing them promptly prevents small issues from developing into systemic weaknesses.

When a non-conformity is identified—whether during an internal audit, surveillance visit, or day-to-day monitoring—the first step is to record it clearly. Each record should describe what happened, the requirement that was not met, the potential impact, and the date discovered. Once logged, a root-cause analysis should be performed to determine why the failure occurred. Understanding the underlying reason is more valuable than fixing the symptom.

The next step is to define and implement corrective actions. These actions must be specific, measurable, and realistic. Each should have an assigned owner, a completion deadline, and defined evidence for verification. Once the corrective actions are completed, a follow-up review confirms that the issue has been resolved and that similar problems are unlikely to recur.

Continuous improvement is an essential outcome of this process. Every resolved non-conformity becomes a learning opportunity. By tracking patterns in findings, organizations can identify areas of weakness, strengthen procedures, and refine controls. Over time, this proactive attitude transforms the ISMS from a compliance mechanism into a dynamic system of organizational learning and risk reduction.

Maintaining openness with auditors about non-conformities also builds trust. Certification bodies expect issues to arise; what matters is how responsibly they are managed. Transparent reporting and evidence of follow-through demonstrate maturity and reinforce confidence in the ISMS.

Conclusion

Achieving ISO 27001 certification represents more than a compliance milestone—it marks the point where information security becomes an integral part of organizational culture. The certification process validates not only the design of the ISMS but also its day-to-day operation, consistency, and commitment to improvement. Once the certificate is earned, the real test begins: sustaining that same level of discipline and effectiveness across years of change, growth, and evolving threats.

Certification should never be seen as a one-time achievement. It signals a continuous promise to stakeholders that the organization values confidentiality, integrity, and availability at every level. Surveillance audits reinforce this promise, ensuring that controls remain effective and that the ISMS adapts as new risks and technologies emerge. Organizations that maintain readiness throughout the year—through internal audits, management reviews, and regular risk updates—rarely struggle with surveillance visits because improvement has become second nature.

The value of certification extends far beyond the certificate itself. It strengthens business reputation, builds client trust, and demonstrates a credible commitment to data protection. Customers, partners, and regulators recognize ISO 27001 as proof of a mature and reliable approach to managing risk. It also promotes internal discipline, helping employees understand that information security is a shared responsibility rather than an isolated department function.

Even in a well-maintained system, non-conformities can appear. How an organization responds to them defines the maturity of its ISMS. Transparent reporting, thorough root-cause analysis, and verified corrective actions show that the organization learns from challenges and uses them to evolve. This continuous feedback loop turns occasional weaknesses into opportunities for lasting improvement.

Thank you for reading.

Protecting information is not just compliance work — it is leadership. If this book helped you take even one real step toward making your organization safer, more trustworthy, and more resilient, then it has done its job.

Stay committed. Keep improving. Security is never finished.

www.ingramcontent.com/pod-product-compliance
Lightning Source LLC
La Vergne TN
LVHW070856210926
843482LV00016B/950
* 9 7 9 8 2 9 5 6 0 3 4 9 5 *